THE
HOMELESS

Opposing Viewpoints®

Other Books of Related Interest in the Opposing Viewpoints Series:

AIDS
American Values
Chemical Dependency
Crime and Criminals
Drug Abuse
Economics in America
The Health Crisis
Poverty
Social Justice
Violence in America

Additional Books in the Opposing Viewpoints Series:

Abortion
American Foreign Policy
American Government
America's Elections
America's Future
America's Prisons
Animal Rights
Biomedical Ethics
Censorship
Central America
China
Civil Liberties
Constructing a Life Philosophy
Criminal Justice
Death and Dying
The Death Penalty
The Elderly
The Environmental Crisis
Euthanasia
Genetic Engineering
Israel
Japan
Latin America and U.S. Foreign Policy
Male/Female Roles
The Mass Media
The Middle East
Nuclear War
The Political Spectrum
Problems of Africa
Religion in America
Science & Religion
Sexual Values
The Soviet Union
The Superpowers: A New Detente
Teenage Sexuality
Terrorism
The Third World
The Vietnam War
War and Human Nature

THE HOMELESS

Opposing Viewpoints®

David L. Bender & Bruno Leone, *Series Editors*

Lisa Orr, *Book Editor*

OPPOSING VIEWPOINTS SERIES ®

Greenhaven Press, Inc.   PO Box 289009   San Diego, CA 92128-9009

Library of Congress Cataloging-in-Publication Data

The Homeless : opposing viewpoints / Lisa Orr, book editor.
  p.   cm. — (Opposing viewpoints series)
  Includes bibliographical references.
  ISBN 0-89908-476-1 — ISBN 0-89908-451-6 (pbk.)
  1. Homelessness—United States. 2. Homeless persons—United States. 3. Homeless persons—Housing—United States. 4. Homelessness—Government policy—United States. I. Orr, Lisa, 1966- . II. Series.
HV4505.H655   1990
362.5'8'0973—dc20   89-25734
                                                            CIP

"Congress shall make no law . . .
abridging the freedom of speech,
or of the press."

First Amendment to the US Constitution

The basic foundation of our democracy is the first amendment guarantee of freedom of expression. The *Opposing Viewpoints Series* is dedicated to the concept of this basic freedom and the idea that it is more important to practice it than to enshrine it.

Contents

Page

Why Consider Opposing Viewpoints?   9
Introduction   13

Chapter 1: Is Homelessness a Serious Problem?

Chapter Preface   16

1. Homelessness Is Serious   17
   Mitch Snyder & Mary Ellen Hombs
2. Homelessness Is Exaggerated   21
   Carl F. Horowitz
3. Homelessness Threatens Working Families   28
   Jonathan Kozol
4. Homelessness Does Not Threaten Working Families   34
   David Whitman
5. Society Should Be Sympathetic Toward the Homeless   39
   James D. Wright
6. Society Should Protect Its Own Interests   46
   John Leo

A Critical Thinking Activity:
Evaluating Sources of Information   50
Periodical Bibliography   52

Chapter 2: What Are the Causes of Homelessness?

Chapter Preface   54

1. Mental Illness Causes Homelessness   55
   H. Richard Lamb & John A. Talbott
2. Mental Illness Does Not Cause Homelessness   60
   Jonathan Kozol
3. Lack of Affordable Housing Causes Homelessness   65
   James D. Wright & Julie A. Lam
4. Family Breakdown Causes Homelessness   71
   Dan McMurry
5. Alcoholism Contributes to Homelessness   75
   Carl I. Cohen & Jay Sokolovsky
6. Economic Factors Cause Homelessness   81
   Peter Marcuse

A Critical Thinking Activity: 88
   Recognizing Statements That Are Provable
Periodical Bibliography   90

Chapter 3: Should the Government Help the Homeless?

Chapter Preface   92
1. The Government Should Do More for the   93
   Homeless
   Peter Marcuse
2. The Government Should Not Do More for the   100
   Homeless
   Kenneth J. Beirne
3. Increasing Welfare Benefits Would Reduce   106
   Homelessness
   Peter Rossi
4. Increasing Welfare Benefits Would Not Reduce   112
   Homelessness
   C. Brandon Crocker
5. The Government Should Support Shelters   117
   Edwin M. Conway
6. Shelters Are Ineffective   123
   Charles Hoch & Robert A. Slayton
7. The Homeless Mentally Ill Should Be   129
   Institutionalized
   Charles Krauthammer
8. The Homeless Mentally Ill Should Not Be   137
   Institutionalized
   Michael J. Dear & Jennifer R. Wolch
A Critical Thinking Activity: 145
   Recognizing Stereotypes
Periodical Bibliography   147

Chapter 4: Can Housing Policies Reduce Homelessness?

Chapter Preface   149
1. A National Housing Policy Would Help the   150
   Homeless
   John I. Gilderbloom & Richard P. Appelbaum
2. A National Housing Policy Would Harm the   156
   Homeless
   Joseph Mehrten

3. Abolishing Rent Control Would Reduce   161
Homelessness
   William Tucker

4. Abolishing Rent Control Would Not Reduce   168
Homelessness
   John Atlas & Peter Dreier

5. The Homeless Should Be Allowed to Occupy   174
Vacant Buildings
   Eric Hirsch & Peter Wood

6. The Homeless Should Not Be Allowed to Occupy   183
Vacant Buildings
   Peter Weber

7. More Public Housing Would Help the Homeless   191
   David C. Schwartz, Richard C. Ferlauto &
   Daniel N. Hoffman

8. Vouchers Would Help the Homeless   197
   Kenneth J. Beirne

A Critical Thinking Activity: 205
Distinguishing Between Fact and Opinion

Periodical Bibliography   207

Organizations to Contact   208
Bibliography of Books   212
Index   213

Why Consider Opposing Viewpoints?

The Importance of Examining Opposing Viewpoints

The purpose of the Opposing Viewpoints Series, and this book in particular, is to present balanced, and often difficult to find, opposing points of view on complex and sensitive issues.

Probably the best way to become informed is to analyze the positions of those who are regarded as experts and well studied on issues. It is important to consider every variety of opinion in an attempt to determine the truth. Opinions from the mainstream of society should be examined. But also important are opinions that are considered radical, reactionary, or minority as well as those stigmatized by some other uncomplimentary label. An important lesson of history is the eventual acceptance of many unpopular and even despised opinions. The ideas of Socrates, Jesus, and Galileo are good examples of this.

Readers will approach this book with their own opinions on the issues debated within it. However, to have a good grasp of one's own viewpoint, it is necessary to understand the arguments of those with whom one disagrees. It can be said that those who do not completely understand their adversary's point of view do not fully understand their own.

A persuasive case for considering opposing viewpoints has been presented by John Stuart Mill in his work *On Liberty*. When examining controversial issues it may be helpful to reflect on this suggestion:

> The only way in which a human being can make some approach to knowing the whole of a subject, is by hearing what can be said about it by persons of every variety of opinion, and studying all modes in which it can be looked at by every character of mind. No wise man ever acquired his wisdom in any mode but this.

Analyzing Sources of Information

The Opposing Viewpoints Series includes diverse materials taken from magazines, journals, books, and newspapers, as well as statements and position papers from a wide range of individuals, organizations and governments. This broad spectrum of sources helps to develop patterns of thinking which are open to the consideration of a variety of opinions.

Pitfalls to Avoid

A pitfall to avoid in considering opposing points of view is that of regarding one's own opinion as being common sense and the most rational stance and the point of view of others as being only opinion and naturally wrong. It may be that another's opinion is correct and one's own is in error.

Another pitfall to avoid is that of closing one's mind to the opinions of those with whom one disagrees. The best way to approach a dialogue is to make one's primary purpose that of understanding the mind and arguments of the other person and not that of enlightening him or her with one's own solutions. More can be learned by listening than speaking.

It is my hope that after reading this book the reader will have a deeper understanding of the issues debated and will appreciate the complexity of even seemingly simple issues on which good and honest people disagree. This awareness is particularly important in a democratic society such as ours where people enter into public debate to determine the common good. Those with whom one disagrees should not necessarily be regarded as enemies, but perhaps simply as people who suggest different paths to a common goal.

Developing Basic Reading and Thinking Skills

In this book, carefully edited opposing viewpoints are purposely placed back to back to create a running debate; each viewpoint is preceded by a short quotation that best expresses the author's main argument. This format instantly plunges the reader into the midst of a controversial issue and greatly aids that reader in mastering the basic skill of recognizing an author's point of view.

A number of basic skills for critical thinking are practiced in the activities that appear throughout the books in the series. Some of the skills are:

Evaluating Sources of Information The ability to choose from among alternative sources the most reliable and accurate source in relation to a given subject.

Separating Fact from Opinion The ability to make the basic distinction between factual statements (those that can be demonstrated or verified empirically) and statements of opinion (those that are beliefs or attitudes that cannot be proved).

Identifying Stereotypes The ability to identify oversimplified, exaggerated descriptions (favorable or unfavorable) about people and insulting statements about racial, religious or national groups, based upon misinformation or lack of information.

Recognizing Ethnocentrism The ability to recognize attitudes or opinions that express the view that one's own race, culture, or group is inherently superior, or those attitudes that judge another culture or group in terms of one's own.

It is important to consider opposing viewpoints and equally important to be able to critically analyze those viewpoints. The activities in this book are designed to help the reader master these thinking skills. Statements are taken from the book's viewpoints and the reader is asked to analyze them. This technique aids the reader in developing skills that not only can be applied to the viewpoints in this book, but also to situations where opinionated spokespersons comment on controversial issues. Although the activities are helpful to the solitary reader, they are most useful when the reader can benefit from the interaction of group discussion.

Using this book and others in the series should help readers develop basic reading and thinking skills. These skills should improve the reader's ability to understand what they read. Readers should be better able to separate fact from opinion, substance from rhetoric and become better consumers of information in our media-centered culture.

This volume of the Opposing Viewpoints Series does not advocate a particular point of view. Quite the contrary! The very nature of the book leaves it to the reader to formulate the opinions he or she finds most suitable. My purpose as publisher is to see that this is made possible by offering a wide range of viewpoints which are fairly presented.

David L. Bender
Publisher

Introduction

"The homeless . . . are homeless, you might say, by choice."
—Ronald Reagan

"The homeless are indeed the most egregious symbol of a cruel economy."
—Robert Hayes, National Coalition for the Homeless

In the late 1960s, sociologists and government officials were predicting a rapid decrease in the number of poor and homeless people in the United States. President Lyndon Johnson, in an effort to continue programs promised by the assassinated John F. Kennedy, had proclaimed a "war on poverty." Johnson initiated reforms that were targeted at the poor and elderly in an effort to eradicate every pocket of poverty.

By the early 1980s, however, it was clear that poverty had not been eliminated. A landmark 1981 study of New York's homeless population by Kim Hopper and Ellen Baxter proved that homelessness was still a serious problem. This study led to a barrage of media attention focused on the homeless problem. Newspapers, magazines, and television began to regularly feature the problem of homelessness.

But do the media give a realistic picture of the homeless problem? Some authorities would answer this question with a resounding yes. For example, in 1987 the Food and Nutrition Service of the U.S. Department of Agriculture estimated that there were between 567,000 and 600,000 homeless people nationwide. This was significantly higher than the 250,000 to 350,000 estimated by the U.S. Department of Housing and Urban Development in 1983. Those who believe these statistics are accurate argue that homelessness is increasing by as much as 38 percent a year. One of the primary reasons given to support this view is that in many cities, shelters have had to turn away dozens of people for lack of space. By the early 1980s, in fact, the world's largest private shelter, The Union Rescue Mission of Los Angeles, had to turn people away for the first time in over ninety years.

But many people disagree that homelessness constitutes a serious national problem. These critics believe that the media and

13

people who work with the homeless exaggerate the problem to fuel public hysteria and concern. Anna Kondratas, administrator of the Food and Nutrition Service of the Department of Agriculture, argues that the media give false credence to advocates' claims by reporting them without questioning them. She believes that the advocates' estimates are much too high, a belief supported by a 1985 study by the Center for Applied Research and Public Policy at the University of the District of Columbia. The Center estimated the number of homeless in the nation at only 7,142, far below the estimates given by other studies. Sociologist Richard Appelbaum, while believing that homelessness has increased, admits that his conviction is based on the claims of "people in the homeless community, who have an axe to grind." Martin Morse Wooster, an associate editor of *The Wilson Quarterly,* makes the point even more strongly. He contends that advocates for the homeless exaggerate the number of homeless people in order to receive more government funding for their shelters and advocacy organizations.

Is there an ever-increasing proportion of poor and disenfranchised people eking out meager lives in the world's most prosperous nation? Or is the problem a reflection of the overactive imaginations of the national media and homeless activists? In *The Homeless: Opposing Viewpoints* these questions are central to the debate. The following topics are covered: Is Homelessness a Serious Problem? What Are the Causes of Homelessness? Should the Government Help the Homeless? and Can Housing Policies Reduce Homelessness? The debate over the seriousness of the homeless problem is seminal to issues concerning government funding, increased housing, and other issues. One thing is certain: Society will continue to struggle with what to do with its poorest members. This anthology is intended to contribute to the debate.

Is Homelessness a Serious Problem?

Chapter Preface

In 1984, the U.S. Department of Housing and Urban Development (HUD) completed a study on the number of people who were homeless in America on any given night. HUD estimated that number to be between 250,000 and 350,000. Mitch Snyder, who leads the homeless activist group Community for Creative Non-Violence, argues that the number is much higher. He believes that a "conservative estimate" would be around three million homeless.

The question of how many people are homeless is central to the debate over the seriousness of the problem. Is homelessness a normal state of affairs for a small segment of the population? Or is it a growing problem affecting thousands of people? The following chapter debates these questions.

*"Our security, and, very possibly, our survival
as a nation may depend on our ability—and
our willingness—to come to grips with . . .
homelessness in America."*

Homelessness Is Serious

Mitch Snyder and Mary Ellen Hombs

Mitch Snyder and Mary Ellen Hombs are members of the Community for Creative Non-Violence, an organization in Washington, D.C. that works to help the homeless. Snyder, a well-known homeless advocate, lives in the organization's shelter. In the following viewpoint, Snyder and Hombs argue that two to three million men, women, and children are homeless nationwide. Many other people are at risk, they argue, since even those who have jobs could lose their homes through one unexpected expense or delayed paycheck. They contend that homelessness should be treated as a national emergency since it is affecting so many people.

As you read, consider the following questions:

1. What do the authors believe causes homelessness?
2. What groups do the authors contend are most likely to become homeless?
3. According to Snyder and Hombs, why haven't people done more for the homeless?

Mitch Snyder and Mary Ellen Hombs, "Sheltering the Homeless: An American Imperative," *State Government: The Journal of State Affairs*, November/December 1986. Reprinted with permission from The Council of State Governments.

From the Skid Row barrios of Los Angeles to the scenic quiet of Vermont, the homeless are all around us. They sleep in the shadows of the White House, under the Dallas freeways, in caves in Appalachia, in shanties in Cincinnati, and in chicken coops in Maine. In suburbs, cities, and in rural America, the homeless are, quite literally, everywhere. Most experts agree that there are 2 to 3 million destitute men, women, and children in our nation competing for fewer than 100,000 shelter beds available to them.

Who are they? Who are these people we see huddled on heat grates or standing in doorways or on street corners?

Paths to Poverty

Although there are as many different reasons for their condition as there are homeless people, there are a few well-travelled paths to destitution:

• The shortage of affordable housing is at crisis proportions. Almost 50 percent of single room occupancy (SRO) housing has been demolished. The Reagan administration radically decreased federal involvement in the creation and maintenance of subsidized housing by reducing funding from $32 billion in 1981 to $9 billion in 1985. The long-term impact is disastrous: It is now commonplace for poor families to face three to ten years on public waiting lists.

• The careless and wholesale depopulation of the nation's mental hospitals has resulted in deinstitutionalizing former patients to the streets or, if they are "lucky," to shelters with insufficient services instead of to community care facilities. The American Psychiatric Association estimates that 1 million or more homeless people in our nation are desperately in need of mental health care.

• The cumulative effects of cuts in federal spending for social programs have driven huge numbers of poor and disabled people to the street. Programs for poor people—constituting 10 percent of the federal budget—were cut almost 30 percent from 1981-83. The effects of those cuts were devastating. For instance, 440,000 families were dropped from Aid to Families with Dependent Children (AFDC) rolls. Supplemental Security Income (SSI) and AFDC do not even bring their recipients close to the established poverty line in most cases. Many eligible people are not reached by food stamps—even though their average payment would be only 49 cents per meal per person if they did get the benefits.

• Unemployment is also a major cause of the dramatic increase in homelessness. The median age of those using soup kitchens and shelters is rapidly dropping (from 56 years of age to 36 in New York City's Bowery, for example, in a two-year period) as members of the labor force—able bodied but unable to find work—join the ranks of the down and out.

18

Getting and keeping a job while homeless is extremely difficult and, once there, escaping the shelters or the street is, for many, nearly impossible. That's why homelessness is often described as akin to getting stuck in quicksand: Once you're there you just can't pull out of it.

• The impact of inflation and recession on the already marginal and those on fixed incomes is also cumulative, decreeing that pensioners, old people, the retired, and the disabled must decide whether "to heat or eat." In 1983, 6.3 million lower-income households spent a majority of their incomes for rent and utilities, up from 3.7 million in 1975. . . . Both the elderly and the working poor stand so near the edge of personal disaster that often only one instance of unexpected circumstance or delayed income will push them over the brink.

A Visible Problem

Homelessness has emerged as the most visible social problem of the 1980s. Homeless persons are evident in virtually every metropolitan area in this country. They sleep on park benches, huddle in doorways, and regularly frequent public libraries during colder weather. City grates offering warm air ventilation are preferred sleeping locations, sometimes necessary for survival. Once closed to the public, certain subway stations become phantom cities for the homeless, at least while local police choose to be tolerant. Homeless persons sleep in cars parked in city, county, and state parks, along abandoned roadways, or in the driveways of family and friends. In colder months, single men, women, and entire family units fill available city shelters to capacity.

Mary E. Stefl, *The Homeless in Contemporary Society*, 1987.

• The breakdown of traditional social structures, relationships, and responsibilities has also meant drastic changes that put many people on the street. For instance, in years past it was unheard of for people to allow their mothers or fathers or grandmothers or grandfathers to live on the street. Now it is commonplace. And chronic poverty itself discourages the formation of families.

Inadequate Response

How has America responded to the phenomenal growth of homelessness from coast to coast? In ways that are neither responsible nor proportionate in their sense of urgency or magnitude.

For example, what do you think would happen if 25,000 or 50,000 New Yorkers were to become homeless because of an earthquake or an explosion or some other natural disaster? Most likely the governor and the mayor would declare a state of emergency. The Red Cross and the Salvation Army would rush in personnel and supplies. School gymnasiums and churches would open their doors. And yet, most experts agree that there are 60,000 or more homeless people in New York City right now—most of them children!

What difference does it make to homeless New Yorkers whether they were driven to destitution because of an earthquake or as a result of unemployment or mental disability? The answer is this: To the homeless it makes no difference at all. It does, however, seem to make a great deal of difference to those who are in a position to do something about it.

Why?

Distance. Distance and ignorance.

Do unto Others

We are very patient with evils like hunger and homelessness because they have not yet touched or affected us, at least not where it counts: not in the depths of our relationships and certainly not in our own flesh.

We must begin to act as though it is our sister or brother, our mother or father, our son or daughter, or we ourselves who huddle silently, shivering in the rain or the cold. . . .

The challenge facing us today is to quickly bring into reality— politically, philosophically, and programmatically—the right of every homeless man, woman, and child in America to adequate and accessible shelter, offered in an atmosphere of reasonable dignity.

Doing More

Although we recognize that government at every level has diminishing resources at its disposal and must work within severe limitations, the elimination of homelessness in America must become national policy. Quickly, as though human lives depended on it, we must create a responsible working model of cooperation, concern, and compassion, that includes every branch of government, the private sector, and the homeless themselves.

While it is evident that no one is doing enough, it is the federal government that has done the least. . . . We must quickly come to grips with federal inaction and indifference, and we must overcome it.

We cannot move into the 21st century with millions of Americans eating out of trash bins and living on the street. Our security, and, very possibly, our survival as a nation may depend on our ability—and our willingness—to come to grips with the contradictions and inconsistencies contained and made manifest by the problem of homelessness in America.

"Advocates for the homeless have made an art form of deflecting questions about their inflated and often absurd estimates."

Homelessness Is Exaggerated

Carl F. Horowitz

In the following viewpoint, Carl F. Horowitz argues that the claim that there are three million homeless people in America is inaccurate. He maintains that advocates for the homeless inflate these figures in order to generate more sympathy for the homeless. In reality, Horowitz contends, reliable surveys have shown in city after city that the homeless population is much smaller than advocates for the homeless suggest. Horowitz is an urban planner in the Washington, D.C., area. He has written several books on housing and planning.

As you read, consider the following questions:

1. What evidence does the author offer that the number of homeless has been exaggerated?
2. What makes the survey that produced the estimate of three million homeless people inaccurate, in Horowitz's opinion?
3. What is the harm of overestimating the number of homeless, according to the author?

"Mitch Snyder's Phony Numbers: The Fiction of Three Million Homeless" by Carl F. Horowitz is reprinted from the Summer 1989 (No. 49) issue of *Policy Review*, the quarterly publication of The Heritage Foundation, 214 Massachusetts Ave. NE, Washington, DC 20002.

Back in the late '70s, homosexual college student organizations developed a novel method of estimating the number of gays on their respective campuses. Often with CETA [Comprehensive Employment and Training Act] funding, their members would fan out at strategic locations throughout campus and count the number of students wearing blue jeans. Before each of these "Blue Jean Days," homosexual students were encouraged to wear jeans as a "consciousness-raising" symbol. But prepublicity was limited, and whoever happened to be wearing jeans on the day of the count was considered homosexual whether he or she actually had any awareness of the "survey." Thus, for example, the homosexual population at Illinois-Urbana was estimated at 45 percent of the student body.

Such a survey was a variation on Senator Joe McCarthy's almost weekly juggling of the number of "known" Communists in the State Department. As the writer Richard Rovere recounted, McCarthy established his original figure of 205 in February 1950, and within months, had revised it in succession to 57, 81, 10, 116, 1, 121, and 106. Too many journalists reported these numbers without scrutinizing his very reputability. The resulting hysteria has undermined serious anti-Communism to this day.

Exaggerated Estimates

In the 1980s, one of the numbers game's premier players has unquestionably been the homeless advocate. Prominent individuals and organizations acting on behalf of the homeless have argued that not simply hundreds of thousands, but millions of Americans on any given day are resigned to a life in shelters, institutions, or the streets. Beginning around 1983, the number three million—approximately 1.2 of every 100 Americans—has come to be reported as the benchmark figure. Politicians, celebrities, and corporations have found it a convenient rallying point to elicit sympathy and tax deductible donations for the homeless. The Washington, D.C., Community for Creative Non-Violence (CCNV) routinely issues the figure in its literature and press releases. Then-House Speaker Jim Wright cited the number three million in the February 1989 Democratic counter-budget speech. Senator Ernest Hollings, in an article in the April 30, 1989, *Washington Post*, "Bush's Real Problem—The Ruins of Reaganism," referred to "upwards of three million" homeless (the title left little doubt as to where he assigns blame). Royal Crown Cola cites the number in conjunction with its campaign to donate part of its profits to homeless organizations. Clergymen lecture from their pulpits about their congregants' duty to help the three million homeless. Cher, Whoopie Goldberg, and Martin Sheen march in the streets for the three million homeless.

The understandable sympathy that Americans feel toward the

22

homeless has effectively limited scrutiny of these estimates. The major media in particular have been guilty of slipshod reporting on this issue, as shown in a survey conducted by the Center for Media and Public Affairs, and cited in the April 19, 1989, *Washington Post*. Researchers monitored 103 CBS, NBC, and ABC evening news stories on the subject over a nearly 30-month period. Only 12 percent of the interviewed homeless adults were unemployed, and only 3 percent were drug or alcohol abusers. This contrasts with a U.S. Conference of Mayors survey indicating that 77 percent of all homeless are unemployed, and 34 percent are substance abusers. The networks quoted homeless advocacy groups more often than federal, state, and local officials combined. Were the networks actually doing their homework, their coverage of the issue would have been quite different.

Western Little Minds

In August 1988, the General Accounting Office (GAO) released *Homeless Mentally Ill: Problems and Options in Estimating Numbers and Trends*, a report that examined 83 national and local studies on the incidence and nature of homelessness, evaluating the soundness of their methods and their utility for future research. Of these studies, only one explicitly or even implicitly claimed a national homeless percentage anywhere near 1.2 percent. *Homelessness: A Forced March to Nowhere*, coauthored in 1982 by Mary Ellen Hombs and Mitch Snyder, and published by Snyder's Community for Creative Non-Violence, consisted of a phone survey of shelter operators across the country.

THE STATE OF SOME PEOPLE

© Al Liederman/Rothco Cartoons

The report states: " . . . in 1980 . . . approximately 1 percent of the population, or 2.2 million people, lacked shelter. We arrived at that conclusion on the basis of information received from more than 100 agencies and organizations in 25 cities and states. It is as accurate an estimate as anyone in the country could offer, yet it lacks absolute statistical certainty." Hombs and Snyder add, "We are convinced the number of homeless people in the United States could reach 3 million or more during 1983."

The monograph, which contained no descriptive methodology that would have shed light on the soundness of its national or local estimates (among other shortcomings), was not one of 27 of the 83 studies considered by the GAO to be "useful." As Anna Kondratas, now an official at the Department of Housing and Urban Development (HUD), noted, the report made no attempt to explain, reconcile, or verify national or local estimates. Some of the estimates were for whole metropolitan areas, others were for cities only; some were point-in-time counts; others were extended period counts. Snyder was refreshingly candid, to say the least, when given the opportunity to explain the figures to a Joint House Committee in May 1984. He admitted, " . . . these numbers are in fact meaningless. We have tried to satisfy your gnawing curiosity for a number because we are Americans with Western little minds that have to quantify everything in sight, whether we can or not."

Growing public outcry over the homelessness issue led HUD to conduct its own analysis. In May 1984 it released the results of a six-month study of homelessness in *A Report to the Secretary on the Homeless and Emergency Shelters.* HUD interviewed 500 local observers in 60 metropolitan areas, visited jails, shelters, and other forms of emergency housing in 10 cities, surveyed 184 shelter operators, and interviewed state officials in all 50 states. HUD also consulted with homeless advocacy groups. The report concluded that the national homeless population (those persons who at night reside in emergency shelters, or in private or public spaces not designated for shelter) ranged from 192,000 to 586,000, with the most reliable range being from 250,000 to 350,000.

HUD's "Nazi Propaganda"

Homeless militants immediately took up cudgels. The numbers were not only drastically low, they argued, they were manipulated to justify Reagan administration domestic budget cuts. *Washington Post* columnist Colman McCarthy accused HUD of "playing games," while Representative Henry Gonzalez, who chaired the Joint House Committee hearings at which Snyder had testified, compared the report to Nazi propaganda. Over four years later, Snyder, still fuming, referred to it on the December 19, 1988, edition of CNN's *Crossfire* as "that stupid study."

But HUD is not the only organization to take exception to Snyder's claim of three million homeless. The CCNV's assertions have been undercut by another homeless advocacy group, the National Alliance to End Homelessness. In 1988, that organization's Alliance Housing Council concluded that there are 735,000 homeless on any given night. And even that figure seems a bit "cooked." The Council reinterpreted and extrapolated from HUD's data, assuming a suburban homeless rate of one-third the city rate, and a 20 percent annual growth in homelessness overall since the HUD study.

Mitch Snyder's Numbers

Mitch Snyder was saying in 1982 that there were three million homeless. Every year since, the advocates and the mayors have been telling us that the numbers have been rapidly increasing, as much as 38 percent a year, but we still have three million homeless. That number was pulled out of the air. It has no relationship to reality, and neither Mitch Snyder nor anyone else has ever produced a shred of evidence to support it, yet newspaper after newspaper, reporting an otherwise perfectly good story on some local problem that really needs addressing, will just pop in these bogus national numbers.

Anna Kondratas, *Rethinking Policy on Homelessness*, 1989.

Other studies also sharply conflict with CCNV estimates. A 1988 National Academy of Sciences book, *Homelessness, Health, and Human Needs*, voices a reasonable critique of the HUD study, but in no way suggests that the number of homeless would have been in the millions had HUD adjusted its sampling methods accordingly. While the book explicitly refrained from providing its own estimates, it implicitly demolished the CCNV report, noting that surveying shelter operators and other service providers (instead of counting the homeless themselves) produces inflated results. The authors elaborated, "The necessity of reliance on the advice of key informants whose perceptions of the size and nature of the homeless population are biased by their own particular set of experiences and who may be unaware of the extent of overlap in service utilization may also badly skew that population estimate.". . .

In late 1988, the Urban Institute released a report, *Feeding the Homeless*, indicating the number of homeless to be between 567,000 and 600,000. Funded by the Agriculture Department's Food and Nutrition Service, the study drew upon more than 1,700 interviews with homeless users of soup kitchens and shelters. Yet although the study arrived at a figure roughly double that of HUD's, and interviewed the "right" people, homeless advocates denounced it. Maria Foscarinis, counsel for the Washington, D.C., National Coalition for the Homeless, responded that the Urban

Institute had vastly miscalculated. "Our estimate is three million," she dryly noted. Mitch Snyder, lending a note of conciliation, remarked, "Just about everybody in America who is involved thinks the figure is two to three million." . . .

Why Numbers Matter

Advocates for the homeless have made an art form of deflecting questions about their inflated and often absurd estimates, either by denying the validity of lower estimates, questioning the competence or the sensitivity of researchers who obtain them, or denying altogether the importance of accurate measurement. As a result, the perception of millions of neglected homeless roaming the streets has gathered wide currency, abetted by a news media that has given advocates a nearly free ride, regularly indulging their grand gestures such as hunger strikes without subjecting their assertions to reasonable scrutiny. This situation is harmful not only to housing policymaking, but to all policymaking.

An inaccurate count of the homeless, high or low, diverts attention from the condition of the people who need help. To devise effective treatment programs for the mentally ill homeless, who account for about one-third of the homeless population, it is essential to know just how many of these tragic individuals there are. The problems of homeless alcoholics are far different from those of homeless mothers with young children, and "advocates" who disparage research about their numbers are doing a serious injustice to the people they ostensibly are trying to aid.

For better or worse, Mitch Snyder's aggressive contempt for facts has set the tenor for the homeless movement. His meteoric rise in stature has been an inspiration for heightened political involvement among an irrational social type for whom strident moral appeals, often tinged with religious symbolism, can and must substitute for good research. Such people reject more than "good data." They reject the very rational-positivist basis of science—that problem definition precedes solution; that facts precede values; and that means and ends are intimately linked. In this sense, Snyder's remark about Americans having "Western little minds" is more than a little self-revealing.

Manipulating Issues

Snyder sounded the opening salvo of a national speaking tour in mid-April 1989, announcing to a church group in Harrisonburg, Virginia, "they [Congress] know we're facing the worst domestic crisis the country has ever faced. And all that stands between that happening and not is money. . . . Affordable housing disappears, because if the federal government doesn't build affordable housing, nobody does." Of course, one might respond that unsubsidized private enterprise has been responsible for most of the more than 12 million housing completions this decade, that the nonprofit sector has initiated successful, low-cost housing rehabilitation programs nationwide, that there were homeless people before HUD's budget cuts, and that a strong economy is still the best defense against a housing depression. Snyder would view making such points as foot-dragging, an excuse for continuing neglect, as the number of homeless climbs to four million, five million, and God-knows-what beyond. Ironically, this manipulation of issues and statistics into a giddy, evasive, and yes, McCarthyist game will do little for the people who most need help: the homeless.

*"The homeless in our midst are no longer
mainly urban hobos and bag ladies. . . .
Joblessness has pushed heretofore self-reliant
families into this subculture."*

Homelessness Threatens Working Families

Jonathan Kozol

Jonathan Kozol is a former teacher and the author of *Illiterate
America, Death at an Early Age,* and several other books about
education and poor children. The following viewpoint is excerpted
from his well-known book on homelessness, *Rachel and Her
Children.* Kozol argues that the old stereotypes of the homeless
are no longer relevant. Today's homeless are not bag ladies or
winos, but families whose breadwinners lost their jobs, he
contends.

As you read, consider the following questions:

1. How would you characterize the homeless families Kozol
   met?
2. What evidence does Kozol cite to show that the number of
   homeless families is increasing?
3. How was the job market changed, according to the author?

Since 1980 homelessness has changed its character. What was once a theater of the grotesque (bag ladies in Grand Central Station, winos sleeping in the dusty sun outside the Greyhound station in El Paso) has grown into the common misery of millions. "This is a new population," said a homeless advocate in Massachusetts. "Many are people who were working all their lives. When they lose their jobs they lose their homes. When they lose their homes they start to lose their families too."

Even in New York City, with its permanent population of the long-term unemployed, 50 percent of individuals served at city shelters during 1984 were there for the first time. The same percentage holds throughout the nation.

Children in Poverty

The chilling fact, from any point of view, is that small children have become the fastest-growing sector of the homeless. At the time of writing there are 28,000 homeless people in emergency shelters in the city of New York. An additional 40,000 are believed to be unsheltered citywide. Of those who are sheltered, about 10,000 are homeless individuals. The remaining 18,000 are parents and children in almost 5,000 families. The average homeless family includes a parent with two or three children. The average child is six years old, the average parent twenty-seven.

In Massachusetts, three fourths of all homeless people are now children and their parents. In certain parts of Massachusetts (Plymouth, Attleboro, and Northampton) 90 to 95 percent of those who have no homes are families with children.

Homeless people are poor people. Four out of ten poor people in America are children, though children make up only one fourth of our population. The number of children living in poverty has grown to 14 million—an increase of 3 million over 1968—while welfare benefits to families with children have declined one third.

Seven hundred thousand poor children, of whom 100,000 have no health insurance, live in New York City. Approximately 20 percent of New York City's children lived in poverty in 1970, 33 percent in 1980, over 40 percent by 1982.

Where Are These People?

They are in midtown Manhattan. They are also in the streets of Phoenix, Salt Lake City, Philadelphia, San Antonio, Miami, and St. Paul. They are in the Steel Belt. They are in the Sun Belt. They are in Kansas City and Seattle. They are in the heartland of America.

In Denver, where evictions rose 800 percent in 1982, hundreds of families were locked on waiting lists for public housing. Many were forced to live in shelters or the streets. In Cleveland, in one classic situation, the loss of a home precipitated by the layoffs in a nearby plant led to the dissolution of a family: the adolescent

29

Susan Blubaugh. Reprinted with permission of *McCall's Magazine*. © 1988 by the Family Circle Inc.

daughter put in foster care, the wife and younger children ending up on welfare, the husband landing in a public shelter when he wasn't sleeping underneath a bridge. Cleveland was obliged to open shelters and soup kitchens in blue-collar neighborhoods that housed traditional white ethnic populations.

The *Milwaukee Journal* wrote: "The homeless in our midst are no longer mainly urban hobos and bag ladies. In recent months, joblessness has pushed heretofore self-reliant families into this subculture." In Michigan, in 1982, the loss of jobs in heavy industry forced Governor Milliken to declare "a state of human emergency"—a declaration other governors may be forced to contemplate.

As an easterner, I had at first assumed that most of these families must be urban, nonwhite, unemployable—perhaps a great deal like the ghetto families I have worked with for much of my life. In 1985, however, I was given an opportunity to visit in over 50 cities and in almost every region of the nation. My hosts were governors and other local politicians, leaders of industry, organizers of the working poor, leaders and advocates of those who recently had joined the unemployed, teachers, school board members, farmers, bankers, owners of local stores. Often they were people who had never met each other and had never even been in the same room with one another, even though they lived in the same towns and cities. They had come together now out of their shared concern over the growth of poverty, the transformation of the labor market, and the rising numbers of those people who no longer could find work at all.

I was invited, in most cases, to address the problems of the public schools. Often, however, education issues became overshadowed by more pressing matters. For many poorly educated people, literacy problems proved of little urgency when they were threatened with the loss of work and loss of home. In a depressed industrial town in Pennsylvania, Lutheran church leaders spoke of the loss of several hundred jobs as truck and auto manufacture left the area and families saw their savings dwindle and their unemployment benefits and pensions disappear while rents rose, food prices climbed, and federal benefits declined.

"Yes, there are new jobs," a minister said. "There's a new McDonald's and a Burger King. You can take home $450 in a month from jobs like that. That might barely pay the rent. What do you do if somebody gets sick? What do you do for food and clothes? These may be good jobs for a teenager. Can you ask a thirty-year-old man who's worked for G.M. since he was eighteen to keep his wife and kids alive on jobs like that? There are jobs cleaning rooms in the hotel you're staying at. Can you expect a single mother with three kids to hold her life together with that kind of work? All you hear about these days are so-called service jobs—it makes me wonder where America is going. If we aren't producing anything of value, will we keep our nation going on hamburger stands? Who is all this 'service' for, if no one's got a real job making something of real worth?"

High Unemployment

In Oklahoma, Arkansas and Texas I met heads of families who had been, only a year or two before, owners of farms, employees of petroleum firms, shopkeepers who supplied the farmers and the oil workers. They had lost their farms, their jobs, their stores. Bankers in Oklahoma City spoke about the rising number of foreclosures. "Oil and agriculture—those are everything for people here. Both are dying. Where will these people go after their farms are boarded and their restaurants and barbershops and hardware stores have been shut down?"

The answers were seen in Phoenix and Los Angeles, where the shelters overflowed and people slept in huge encampments on the edges of the seamy areas of town. In one city homeless families lived in caves. I went out to visit. I had never seen a family living in a cave before.

In Portland, Oregon, the governor told me of some counties in which unemployment caused by the declining lumber industry had climbed above 30 percent. Where did the lumber workers go? I met some of them the same night in a homeless shelter by the Burnside Bridge. A pregnant woman and her husband spoke to me while waiting for the soup line to be formed. "We had good work until last year. Since then we've had no home. Our kids were put in foster care." They had been sleeping on a plywood plank supported by the girders of the bridge. The traffic was two feet above their heads.

Earnings Fall Short

"They are the new homeless," says Maria Foscarinis, a lawyer with the National Coalition for the Homeless, a federation of advocacy groups based in Washington. "We're seeing many more intact families who can't find housing they can afford."

These families are not made up of drifters. More than one-fifth of our homeless are employed. Very often they are working parents—one or both of whom hold jobs. But their combined earnings never total a month's rent and a matching security deposit with enough left to buy food.

Hank Whittemore, *Parade*, January 10, 1988.

"The sound of the trucks puts me to sleep at night," she said. I learned that even makeshift housing space under the bridge was growing scarce.

In San Antonio I met a father with two boys who had been sleeping for four months next to the highway not far from the Hyatt Regency Hotel. He sold blood plasma twice a week to buy food for his kids. "They draw my blood, put it in a centrifuge, take the white cells, and inject the red cells back into my arm." If he showed up four weeks straight he got a bonus. In a good month he made $100. "The blood places," he told me, "poor people call them 'stab labs.' They're all over." He showed me a card he carried listing stab labs, with phone numbers and addresses, in a dozen cities. He had been an auto worker in Detroit. When he lost his job his wife became depressed and since was hospitalized. He had developed crippling asthma—"from the panic and the tension, I believe." He had thought mistakenly that San Antonio might offer health and labor and cheap housing that were not available in Michigan.

In Miami I met a woman, thirty-five years old, from Boston. She

32

had attended Girls' Latin, the same high school that my mother had attended. After graduation she had gone to college and had worked for many years until she was the victim of a throat disease that led to complications that wiped out her savings, forced her to lose her home, ended her marriage, and at last compelled her to give up her kids. She'd moved to Miami hoping it would help her health but couldn't cope with illness, loss of family, loss of home—and now was sleeping on Miami Beach.

She had a tube in her stomach to bypass her damaged throat. At a shelter run by Catholic brothers she would pulverize the food, mix it with water, and inject the liquid mix into her tube.

In New York I spoke with Robert Hayes, counsel to the National Coalition for the Homeless. Hayes and his co-workers said that three fourths of the newly homeless in America are families with children.

In Washington, D.C., in late September 1986, I spent an afternoon with the director of a shelter, Sandy Brawders, one of those saints and martyrs of whom Robert Hayes has said, only half-jokingly, the homeless movement is primarily composed. ("There are the saints," he says, "and then there are the martyrs who have to put up with the saints.") Sandy told me that the homeless population was exploding in the District; the largest growth in numbers was among young children and their parents.

Four months later, the *Washington Post* reported that the number of homeless families in the District had increased 500 percent in just one year and that there were 12,000 people on a waiting list for public housing, with a waiting period of more than seven years.

Even at Home

Home in New England in a small town north of Boston, I shared some of these stories with a woman who works at the counter of a local grocery. "You didn't have to go to San Antonio and Florida," she said. "There's hundreds of homeless families just a couple miles from here." When I asked her where, she said: "In Ipswich, Gloucester, Haverhill. . . . There are families who are living in the basement of my church." After a moment's pause she told me this: "After my husband lost his job—we had some troubles then, I was divorced . . . I had to bring my family to the church. . . . Well, we're still there."

"The old stereotypes were pretty close to the truth . . . a hefty majority of the homeless are still alcoholics, drug addicts, or mentally ill."

Homelessness Does Not Threaten Working Families

David Whitman

The media are focusing on working families who lose their homes in order to make the public more sympathetic to the homeless, according to David Whitman. In the following viewpoint, he argues that most of the homeless are mentally ill, alcoholics, or drug addicts, not parents who lose jobs. Whitman is an associate editor of *U.S. News & World Report*.

As you read, consider the following questions:

1. How does the media distort the image of the homeless, according to the author?
2. Why does Whitman believe families become homeless?
3. How does the author contend media reports have affected public opinion?

David Whitman, "Who's Who Among the Homeless," *The New Republic*, June 6, 1988. Reprinted by permission of THE NEW REPUBLIC, © 1988, The New Republic, Inc.

In January of 1988 the *New Yorker* published generous chunks of *Rachel and Her Children*, Jonathan Kozol's book about the struggles of homeless families in a New York City welfare hotel. Since then all three CBS newsmagazines have devoted special segments to homeless youth and homeless families. ABC ran "God Bless the Child," a made-for-TV movie about a homeless mother and her young daughter. And not to be outdone, NBC aired "Home Sweet Home," a one-hour special that spotlighted the urgent plight of homeless families in Iowa.

Kozol's book and these reports vividly convey how the shelter system tears apart homeless families and saps their initiative. But in seeking to make the homeless more palatable to the public, they present a distorted picture of how mothers and children end up on the street. The prevailing diagnosis of homeless families, as Mike Wallace put it in a "60 Minutes" segment on the middle-class homeless, is that "these are people who are simply, suddenly poor. They cannot pay the rent, they cannot find a place to live." In virtually all of the TV reports and docudramas, homeless mothers are portrayed as white, working-class, and—above all—victims. (On "Nightline" Kozol went so far as to liken homeless families to concentration camp inmates.) In fact, the "there but for the grace of God go I" analysis that Kozol, Wallace, and others employ is phony. As a result the public is repeatedly misled about what kind of help families need to return to homes of their own.

The Real Homeless

Every study of homeless families in urban areas shows that the majority are black or Hispanic, on welfare, and headed by a single mother. Though Tom Brokaw opened the NBC special by stating, "This is a program about people you know," homeless families actually are very rare, even among the poor. One of the few surveys so far in which researchers actually went out into the streets and shelters to count the homeless found that less than three percent of Chicago's poorest single adults end up homeless on a given night. The comparable figure for poor families—who make up about a third of the homeless—is even lower.

Besides being a tiny subsection of the poor, homeless families are often deeply troubled long before they lose their apartments. The most detailed study of homeless families, done in 14 Massachusetts family shelters by Harvard professor Ellen Bassuk, shows that many homeless mothers tend to be lousy parents who were abused by their own mothers. Roughly a quarter of the women surveyed had been investigated for child abuse and neglect; a quarter had a major psychiatric problem resulting from substance abuse or a mental disorder; and over 40 percent of the children had repeated a grade *before* arriving at the shelter. Most of the mothers had never worked or had held a job only sporadically. As a 1986 congressional committee report on homeless families put it, "Many of these [women] exhibit an inability to function as adults."

Thus anyone doing an in-depth report on homeless families, as Kozol attempted, has to talk to some very disturbed mothers. In his introduction to *Rachel and Her Children*, he acknowledges that his welfare hotel includes families with alcoholics, mentally ill, prostitutes, drug addicts, and drug dealers. But he barely mentions them. And for the families he does include, he minimizes any discussion of substance abuse and psychiatric problems that may have led them to be thrown out onto the street. Such matters are "ancillary aspects of the fact of homelessness."

Deceiving the Public

If you go to a typical congressional hearing . . . very often the homeless individuals who are brought to the hearings are purposely atypical. A two-parent, white family with children from a small town will elicit a great deal of public sympathy because the middle class can identify with it, but it is not the typical homeless family and even less representative of the vast majority of homeless individuals. Not that such people do not exist, but they are not typical and do not represent a trend. So the public is deceived to further a political agenda. If there is no true understanding of the problem, and a total misconception about the numbers, bad policy is the result.

Anna Kondratas, *The Heritage Lectures: Rethinking Policy on Homelessness*, 1989.

Kozol is ultimately so afraid of "blaming the victim" that he evades the key policy question: Why do three percent of the poor end up homeless when 97 percent don't? The answer, as Bassuk's and other studies show, is that homeless women typically have few, if any, close family members and friends. They often react to a personal or financial emergency by "doubling-up" with a relative or friend. But their ties are so fragile that they end up in a shelter. "These mothers have horrible support systems," says Bassuk. "And you don't develop that by accident. A lot of them get caught up with terrible men who drink and batter them."

A Homogenized View

That disturbing picture rarely reaches the public, thanks to the homogenized analysis of homeless advocates, reporters, and politicians. The homeless advocates' interest is obvious: they fear the homeless will receive aid only if they are deemed "deserving." As Maria Foscarinis of the National Coalition for the Homeless puts it: "Homelessness among families is merely one further confirmation that the homeless population now mirrors the national population."

Reporters have their own reasons for holding a cracked mirror up to the public. Any reporter who has talked with homeless families knows a shelter director will steer him to the most articulate, well-adjusted mother for an interview—someone who did just lose her apartment because she couldn't afford the rent increase. And the reporter often *asks* for just such a prescreening. In 1987 I wrote an article about how the shortage of low-income housing contributed to the growth in homeless families. I was delighted, I confess, to see that most shelter directors could find at least one eviction horror story.

The same is true for those with a political agenda. As Robert Hayes of the National Coalition for the Homeless acknowledged to *Fortune*: "I can't tell you how often a congressional committee has called and said, 'We need a witness for a hearing. Can you get us a homeless family: mother, father—father out of work in the past four months from an industrial plant—white?'"

In one sense the new interest in homeless families is welcome. It counteracts the myth that the homeless are all deinstitutionalized mental patients. The most complete breakdown of today's homeless comes from an ongoing 18-city National Institute of Mental Health demonstration project that helped 11,000 homeless individuals in its first year of operation. The results show considerable heterogeneity: only a third of the homeless were mentally ill (the same number that city officials estimated in a U.S. Conference of Mayors survey); 40 percent were alcoholics; and roughly 15 percent were drug abusers. Since there is some double counting, a fair estimate is that two-thirds of the homeless are either mentally ill or substance abusers, and between a quarter and a third are families.

The New Myth

Yet in erasing the old myth, journalists have created a new one: that most of the homeless are families in need of apartments. *Newsweek* ran a piece called "What Can Be Done?" offering suggestions for solving the homeless problem. The first tip was that we must "drop old stereotypes" because "studies suggest that [the mentally ill, alcoholics, and drug addicts] add up to less than half of the total homeless population." I called Tom Mathews, *Newsweek*'s writer, to ask what studies he was referring to. He said that the U.S. Conference of Mayors' annual 26-city survey showed that the mentally ill and substance abusers added up to 58 percent of the homeless population. (Actually it was 61 percent.) That figure "seemed a little high," so he called the Washington office of the National Coalition for the Homeless, which said that only 40 percent of the homeless were mentally ill or substance abusers. "It's working very imprecisely with statistics," he acknowledged. "But I was making an educated estimate based on two estimates that straddle 50 percent by eight to ten points."

Wild Guesses

One problem with that estimate: the 40 percent figure turns out to be a wild guess made by a National Coalition staff member. Tim Hager, the assistant director of the Coalition's Washington office, admits he can't cite any studies to back up the number—and adds that in its own surveys the Coalition asks its affiliates only to guess the percent of homeless that are working or part of families. Yet stories like *Newsweek's* have swayed public assessments of the homeless. In 1986 a CBS/*New York Times* poll showed only 19 percent of the public believed bad economic luck caused people to become homeless. A national poll taken in January 1988 showed a majority now believes most of the homeless are victims of a "tough economic situation beyond their control."

The real truth, however unpleasant, is that the old stereotypes were pretty close to the truth. Despite the upsurge in homeless families in the past several years, a hefty majority of the homeless are still alcoholics, drug addicts, or mentally ill. And it's not homeless families, but homeless alcoholics, who are largely ignored. About three out of four homeless alcoholics come out of detox without any referral for aftercare. Yet educating the public on such matters isn't easy. After all, who wants to sit through a TV movie about a destitute drunk?

"In puzzling through the complex array of factors that cause homelessness, in the hopes of finding some solutions, coldheartedness is not the proper sentiment."

Society Should Be Sympathetic Toward the Homeless

James D. Wright

James D. Wright is the Charles and Leo Favrot Professor of Human Relations in the sociology department at Tulane University in New Orleans, Louisiana. A prolific writer, in 1987 he co-authored *Homelessness and Health*. In the following viewpoint, Wright examines what he maintains is the common belief that the homeless are divided into two groups: those who are worthy of our sympathy, and those who are shiftless and deserve contempt. Wright contends that only a negligible percentage of the homeless fit the stereotype of lazy, unemployed people who could be considered contemptible. Most homeless, he writes, are families whose breadwinner suddenly lost a job, or mentally or physically handicapped people who cannot work. Thus he concludes that society should view the homeless with compassion.

As you read, consider the following questions:

1. Why does Wright believe that homeless families deserve our sympathy?
2. Why do homeless teenagers need sympathy, even if they are involved in drugs or crime, according to the author?

James D. Wright, "The Worthy and the Unworthy Homeless," *Society*, July/August 1988. Published by permission of Transaction Publishers, from SOCIETY, Vol. 25, No. 5. Copyright © 1988 by Transaction Publishers.

Americans have always found it necessary to distinguish between the "deserving" and "undeserving" poor—the former, victims of circumstances beyond their control who merit compassion; the latter, lazy, shiftless bums who could do better for themselves "if they wanted to" and who therefore merit contempt. . . .

A Heartless Response

So far, the homeless seem to be included among the "deserving poor," at least by the general public. A national survey by the Roper Organization reported by *Newsweek* on September 21, 1987, asked what problems we should be spending more money on. "Caring for the homeless" was the top priority item, favored by 68 percent. (In contrast, foreign aid was mentioned by only 5 percent, and "military, armaments, and defense" by only 17 percent.) Thus, most people seem to feel that the homeless deserve our help, if not our compassion. But an opposite, more mean-spirited view has also begun to surface. On December 1, 1986, Stuart Bykofsky wrote a "My Turn" column for *Newsweek* magazine entitled "No Heart for the Homeless." The analysis turned on the division of the homeless into three groups: "(1) the economically distressed, who would work if they could find work; (2) the mentally ill, who can't work; (3) the alcoholic, the drug-addicted, and others who won't work." His solution to the problem was workfare for the first group, mental institutions for the second, and indifference to (or outright hostility toward) the third.

Bykofsky's simplistic categorization was unburdened by numbers or percentages, and so we are not told how many of the homeless fit his various types. Concurrent with the increased media and political attention being given to the problem, there has also been an outpouring of research studies that provide reliable guides to the relative proportions of "worthy" and "unworthy" homeless. My aim here is to review the findings of some of these studies, to see if we cannot be more precise about how many homeless deserve our sympathies and how many do not. . . .

For convenience, it is useful to begin by imagining a sample of 1,000 homeless people, drawn at random, let us say, from the half million or so homeless people to be found in America on any given evening. Based on the research I have sketched, we can then begin to cut up this sample in various ways, so as to portray as graphically as possible the mosaic of homelessness in this country. Our strategy is to work from "more deserving" to "less deserving" subgroups, ending with the absolutely least deserving—the lazy, shiftless bums. Along the way, I call attention to various characteristics of and problems encountered by each of the subgroups we consider.

Among the many tragedies of homelessness, there is none sadder than the homeless family—often an intact family unit consisting of a wife, her husband, and one or more dependent children, victims of unemployment and other economic misfortune, struggling in the face of long odds to maintain themselves as a unit and get back on their feet again. How many members of homeless families can we expect to find among our sample of 1,000 homeless people? . . .

© Adair/Rothco Cartoons

Members of homeless families constitute a significantly large fraction of the homeless population; my guess is that we would find 220 of them in a sample of a thousand homeless people, nearly half of them homeless children. Not only would most people look on homeless families as most deserving of help, there is also reason to believe that they need the least help (in that they appear to have the fewest disabling problems and tend generally to be the most intact), and that even relatively modest assistance would make a substantial difference in their life chances and circumstances. If the available resources are such as to require triage, then homeless families should be the top priority.

Lone Women and Children

By these calculations, there remain in our hypothetical sample of 1,000 some 780 lone homeless persons—single individuals on the streets by themselves. Based on the HCH [National Health Care for the Homeless Program] study, some 6 percent of these

780 are children or adolescents age nineteen or less (which amounts to 47 additional children in the sample of 1,000), 20 percent are adult women (156 additional women), and 74 percent are adult men (which leaves, from the original sample of 1,000, only 580 adult males not members of homeless family groups). Adding these to the earlier results, we get two significant conclusions: First, among the total of a thousand homeless persons, 99 + 47 = 146 will be children or youths aged nineteen or less, approximately one in every seven. Second, among the remaining 854 adults, 156 + 83 = 229 will be women, which amounts to 229/854 or 27 percent of all adults. Combining all figures, homeless children and homeless adult women themselves comprise 146 + 229 = 375 of the original 1,000—three of every eight. Adult men comprise the majority of the homeless, but not the overwhelming majority; a very sizable minority—nearly 40 percent of the total—are women and children. . . .

Although precise numbers are hard to come by, there is little doubt that many of these homeless teenagers are runaway or throwaway children fleeing abusive family situations. Among the girls, the rate of pregnancy is astonishing: 9 percent of the girls ages thirteen to fifteen, and 24 percent of the girls ages sixteen to nineteen, were pregnant at or since their first contact with the HCH clinic system; the rate for sixteen-to-nineteen-year-olds is the highest observed in any age-group. There is impressionistic evidence, but no hard evidence, to suggest that many of these young girls are reduced to prostitution in order to survive; many will thus come to possess lengthy jail records as well. Drug and alcohol abuse are also common problems. Indeed, the rate of known drug abuse among the sixteen-to-nineteen-year-old boys—some 16 percent—is the highest rate recorded for any age-group in our data.

Unending Worries

I am discussing a time in life when the average adolescent's biggest worries are acne, or whom to invite to the high school prom, or where to go to college—a time of uncertainty, but also a time of hope and anticipation for the future. In contrast, homeless adolescents must worry about where to sleep tonight, or where the next meal is coming from, or who is going to assault them next. What hope for the future can be nourished under these conditions? Many of these kids—tough kids on mean streets, but kids nonetheless—face an unending downward spiral of booze, drugs, crime, and troubles with the law. They too must surely be counted among the "deserving" homeless; indeed, anything that can be done should be done to break the spiral and set them back on a path to an independent and productive adult existence. . . .

Most people would feel comfortable counting the adult women among the "deserving" homeless as well. Just as women and children are the first to be evacuated from a sinking ship, so too should women and children be the first to be rescued from the degradations of street life or a shelter existence. If we add to the group of "deserving" homeless the relatively small number of adult men in homeless family groups, then our initial cut leaves but 580 persons from the original 1,000 yet to account for.

Lone Adult Men

What is to be said about those who remain—the 580 lone adult males, not members of homeless families? A small percentage of them, much smaller than most people would anticipate, are elderly men, over age sixty-five; in the HCH data, the over-sixty-fives comprise about 3 percent of the group in question, which gives us 17 elderly men among the remaining 580. . . .

Distancing the Homeless

The homeless are a nightmare. . . . It is natural to fear and try to banish nightmares. It is not natural to try to banish human beings.

The distancing receives its most extreme expression in the use of language such as "undeserving." This is, in some sense, the ultimate act of disaffiliation and the most decisive means of placing all these families and their children in a category where they can't intrude upon our dreams.

Jonathan Kozol, *Rachel and Her Children*, 1988.

Those over sixty-five surely are to be included within the "deserving" group. As it happens, only about half of them receive Social Security benefits. Many of those who do receive Social Security payments find that no housing can be purchased or rented within their means. Well over half have chronic physical health problems that further contribute to their hardships. Certainly, no one will object if we include the elderly homeless among those deserving our sympathies.

Lone Veterans

We are now left with, let us say, 563 nonelderly lone adult men. If we inquire further among this group, we will discover another surprising fact: at least a third of them are veterans of the United States Armed Forces. . . .

Most homeless veterans are drawn from the lower socioeconomic strata, having enlisted to obtain, as M. Robertson has put it, "long term economic advantages through job training as well as postmilitary college benefits and preferential treatment in civil service employment," only to find that their economic and employment opportunities remain limited after they have mustered out.

The lure of military service proves to have been a false promise for many of these men: "Despite recruitment campaigns that promote military service as an opportunity for maturation and occupational mobility, veterans continue to struggle with postmilitary unemployment and mental and physical disability without adequate assistance from the federal government." One of the Vietnam veterans in Robertson's study summed up the stakes involved: "If they expect the youth of America to fight another war, they have to take care of the vets."

Many of the homeless veterans are alcoholic or drug abusive, and many are also mentally ill; the same could be said for other subgroups that we have considered. Whatever their current problems and disabilities, these men were there when the nation needed them. Do they not also deserve a return of the favor?

Lone Disabled Men

Sticking with the admittedly conservative one-third estimate, among the 563 adult men with whom we are left, 188 will be veterans; 375 nonelderly, nonveteran adult men are all that remain of the initial 1,000. Sorting out this subgroup in the HCH data, we find that a third are assessed by their care providers as having moderate to severe psychiatric impairments—not including alcohol or drug abuse. Many among this group have fallen through the cracks of the community mental health system. In the vast majority of cases, they pose no immediate danger to themselves or to others, and thus they are generally immune to involuntary commitment for psychiatric treatment; at the same time, their ability to care for themselves, especially in a street or shelter environment, is at best marginal. Compassion dictates that they too be included among the "deserving" group. . . .

Subtracting the 125 or so mentally disabled men from the remaining group of 375 leaves 250 of the original 1,000. Among these 250 will be some 28 or so men who are physically disabled and incapable of working. This includes the blind and the deaf, those confined to wheelchairs, the paraplegic, those with amputated limbs, and those with disabling chronic physical illnesses such as heart disease, AIDS, obstructive pulmonary disease, and others. Like the mentally disabled, these too can only be counted among the "deserving" group. Subtracting them leaves a mere 222 remaining—nonelderly, nonveteran adult males with no mental or physical disability.

Of these 222, a bit more than half—112 men—will be found to have some sort of job: my data suggest that 7 will have full-time jobs, 27 will have part-time jobs, and 78 will be employed on a sporadic basis (seasonal work, day labor, odd jobs, and the like). Peter Rossi's Chicago data show largely the same pattern. The remainder—110 men—are unemployed, and among these some

61 will be looking for work. All told, then, among the 222 will be 173 who are at least making the effort: looking for work, but so far with no success, or having a job but not one paying well enough to allow them to afford stable housing. This then leaves us with 49 people from the initial 1,000 who are not members of homeless families, not women, not children, not elderly, not veterans, not mentally disabled, not physically disabled, not currently working, and not looking for work. Call these the "undeserving homeless," or, if you wish, lazy shiftless bums. They account for about 5 percent of the total—a mere one in every twenty. . . .

Avoiding Indifference

In puzzling through the complex array of factors that cause homelessness, in the hopes of finding some solutions, cold-heartedness is not the proper sentiment. Should we, as Bykofsky suggests, have "no heart" for a disabled thirty-three-year-old Vietnam veteran suffering from posttraumatic stress syndrome, or for a pregnant fifteen-year-old runaway girl whose father has raped and beaten her once too often, or for a feverish infant in the arms of her homeless mother, or for an entire family that has been turned out because the factory where the father worked was shut down, or for an arthritic old gentleman who has lost his room in the "welfare hotel" because he was beaten savagely and relieved of his Social Security check? These are very much a part—a large part—of today's homeless population, no less than the occasional "shiftless bum." Indifference to the plight of "shiftless bums" comes all too easily in an illiberal era; but indifference to the plight of homeless families, women, children, old people, veterans, and the disabled comes easily only to the cruel.

"The homeless should not be allowed to destabilize the live communities still left in our cities."

Society Should Protect Its Own Interests

John Leo

In the following viewpoint, John Leo argues that the rights of the community are not given sufficient consideration in discussions of the homeless problem. Leo believes that homeless people harm communities by contributing to the deterioration of neighborhoods. The presence of the homeless in city parks keeps other citizens away, he writes, and eventually leads to criminals taking over the parks. Leo writes for *Reader's Digest, New York,* and *U.S. News & World Report.*

As you read, consider the following questions:

1. Why do homeless advocates ignore the rights of the community, in the author's opinion?
2. What is Leo's opinion of New York City's attempt to halt the deterioration of city parks?
3. Why does Leo believe homeless camps are a problem?

Read a few reports or books on the problem of the homeless, and chances are that in the index, under the letter C, you will find "compassion" and "causes, root," but not "community, rights of."

The reason for this is that the left, which is producing almost all the programs dealing with the growing army of street people, has no tradition at all of thinking about community, towns and neighborhoods. As always, the Achilles' heel of liberalism is its reflexive tendency to convert every social or moral or political problem into a dramatic confrontation between a beleaguered individual and the all-powerful, menacing state. The community is nowhere to be found.

Destabilizing Communities

Each winter, when winos and addicts sleep over the hot-air grates on streets and subways, and apartment dwellers have to step over bodies to get out the door, there is (and should be) much compassion for the disoriented street people. This will lead to discussion of the presumed "right" to sleep wherever one collapses, and the argument that this behavior "does not harm anyone." But there will be no discussion about the demoralization of the neighbors or the connection between the loss of social controls and the destabilization of entire communities. If anyone brings up the point, he will be portrayed as a heartless "have" intent on abusing the "have-nots."

Each spring, the army migrates to the parks, where the destabilization process often seems to work even faster. Sandboxes become urinals. Swings are broken. Every park bench seems to be owned by a permanently curled-up dozing alcoholic or perhaps a street schizophrenic. When the cycle is complete, the community withdraws, serious druggies and criminals move in, and you have what Los Angeles and Washington, D.C., are now calling "dead parks." This cycle can occur without the homeless—the criminals can move directly into a live park and kill it—but only in neighborhoods already softened up by the destabilization process. And today that destabilization is very likely to be spearheaded by the homeless street people.

Napping Campers

New York City is trying to halt the process of deterioration in the parks, within the constraints of a political culture notably blind to community and obsessed by individual rights. This is like wrestling a greased pig blindfolded, but at least the effort is being made. In 1988, the city's parks commissioner proposed regulations against panhandling ("soliciting money"), annoying other people and lying down on park benches for more than 2 hours. "What about Girl Scouts soliciting money for their cookies?" someone asked, so that provision was dropped. "What about a

Wall Street broker napping for 2 hours and 1 minute on a park bench?'' someone else asked, so the provision was relaxed to allow longer sleeping periods, but not camping without a permit. "Isn't this a mean-spirited attempt to exclude the homeless?'' yet another concerned citizen asked, so the parks department apologized for "the insensitivity'' of its language, and the parks commissioner insisted, with a straight face, that the rules were not aimed at the homeless at all.

Downtown, in Tompkins Square Park on the Lower East Side, the parks department showed more spine, but then more is at stake. The street people, egged on by an assortment of ax grinders, from dreamy revolutionaries to skinheads, set up what appeared to be a permanent shantytown in the park. Inhabitants included poor people gentrified out of nearby apartments, as well as derelicts, assorted hustlers, drug dealers and the mentally ill. This little community featured the predictable sanitation problems, frequent theft and one full-time brothel.

The Living Nightmare

I am about to be heartless. There are people living on the streets of most American cities, turning sidewalks into dormitories. They are called the homeless, street people, vagrants, beggars, vent men, bag ladies, bums. Often they are called worse. They are America's living nightmare—tattered human bundles. They have got to go.

I don't know, exactly, when they got the *right* to live on the street. I don't know, exactly, when I *lost* the right to walk through town without being pestered by panhandlers. I do know I want them off my sidewalk. If you think I am heartless for saying that, can I send them to live on *your* sidewalk?

I am fed up with the trash they bring into my neighborhood. The pools of urine in apartment-house lobbies disgust me. I am fed up with picking my way down sidewalks blocked by plastic milk crates, stepping over human forms sprawled on steam gratings.

I also am fed up with newspaper columnists who periodically have a good cry in print over the plight of the street people—and the average citizen's callous reaction to them. I have yet to read that one of these columnists has taken a street person home for a bath and a meal. That happens only in movies like "Down and Out in Beverly Hills.''

Stuart D. Bykofsky, *Newsweek*, December 1, 1986.

On order from the parks department, police tore down the shacks and tents. The squatters put them up again. Both sides have promised nonviolence (during the summer of 1988, police went berserk and cracked heads at random), so the police will politely keep tearing down the tents, and the squatters will politely keep putting them back up. This silly arrangement, which could have come from a Chaplin comedy, makes the city's paralysis painfully obvious. The administration won't back down, but it won't clear the park, either.

A Conventionally Liberal Clash

The "heartlessness" refrain is obscuring the very sensible principle that the parks department is trying to uphold, which is that parks are for recreation, not human habitation. The city maintains a huge system of shelters for the homeless and spends more on this safety net than all other large American cities combined, offering food, clothing, social services and medical care.

Leaders of the homeless deride the shelters as unsafe and unclean (i.e., they are filled with homeless people, who bring their habits and problems with them). But instead of pushing for even more guards—security costs at the shelters are already up to $57 million a year—these leaders have reframed the issue as a conventionally liberal clash between a heartless government and beleaguered victims rightly refusing to be regimented. Posing the problem in that manner is a sure-fire way of making it insoluble.

The homeless deserve food and shelter. Certainly, a country as rich as this can afford it. But the homeless should not be allowed to destabilize the live communities still left in our cities. James Q. Wilson's book *Thinking About Crime* has the best discussion of how disordered street life eats away at the informal controls that hold a community together, even before a single street crime has been committed. Muggers and robbers flourish on streets where potential victims are already intimidated by prevailing conditions. The first step to reclaiming a street, or a park, is to change those prevailing conditions.

Evaluating Sources
of Information

A critical thinker must always question sources of information. Historians, for example, distinguish between *primary sources* (eyewitness accounts) and *secondary sources* (writings or statements based on primary or eyewitness accounts or on other secondary sources). A description of homelessness given by a single mother who has lived on the streets for a year with her two children is an example of a primary source. A sociologist writing a book on homeless families using the homeless mother's description is an example of a secondary source.

To read and think critically, one must be able to recognize primary sources. This is not enough, however, because eyewitness accounts do not always provide accurate descriptions. A homeless mother's account of life in a shelter may differ from the account of the shelter's operator. The sociologist must decide which account seems most accurate, keeping in mind the potential biases of the eyewitnesses.

Test your skill in evaluating sources of information by completing the following exercise. Imagine you are writing a paper on whether homelessness is a serious problem in America. You decide to include an equal number of primary and secondary sources. Listed below are a number of sources which may be useful for your research. *Place a P next to those descriptions you believe are primary sources.* Second, *rank the primary sources* assigning the number (1) to what appears to be the most accurate and fair primary source, the number (2) to the next most accurate, and so on until the ranking is finished. Next, *place an S next to those descriptions you believe are secondary sources and rank them also, using the same criteria.*

If you are doing this activity as a member of a class or group, discuss and compare your evaluation with other members of the group.

P = *primary*
S = *secondary*

_____ 1. An interview with a priest who runs a shelter for homeless children. He turns children away because the shelter lacks room for all the needy children.   _____

_____ 2. A study done by the federal housing authority summarizing the reasons for the skyrocketing costs of public housing in cities on the West Coast.   _____

_____ 3. A videotaped interview of twelve homeless men in New York City's Bowery, in which the men discuss how and why they ended up on the streets.   _____

_____ 4. A book discussing the needs, hopes, and dreams of homeless children written by a now-successful businesswoman who spent three years living on the streets as a homeless teenager.   _____

_____ 5. A report on ABC's "World News Tonight" that includes a government official's comment that the only homeless people he knows are shiftless bums who only have themselves to blame because they are too lazy to work for a living.   _____

_____ 6. A public television documentary in which the owner of a flophouse on Chicago's skid row talks about his fifteen years of experience with the homeless residents that have frequented his establishment.   _____

_____ 7. A U.S. Census Bureau report on the numbers of homeless people in America based on the use of publicly funded shelters during the previous year.   _____

_____ 8. Your personal interview with a homeless old woman who sleeps in the park near your house.   _____

Periodical Bibliography

The following articles have been selected to supplement the diverse views presented in this chapter.

Chris Anderson	"How Many Are Homeless?" *Utne Reader,* January/February 1988.
Lyn Cryderman	"Harder to Ignore?" *Christianity Today,* November 18, 1988.
Don Feder	"Let's Stop Romanticizing the Homeless," *Conservative Chronicle,* February 8, 1989. Available from *Conservative Chronicle,* Box 29, Hampton, IA 50441.
David Hilfiker	"Are We Comfortable with Homelessness?" *Journal of the American Medical Association,* September 8, 1989.
Barry Jacobs	"Under the Boardwalk," *The Progressive,* October 1987.
Thomas J. Main	"What We Know About the Homeless," *Commentary,* May 1988.
D. Keith Mano	"Homeless in New York," *National Review,* October 9, 1987.
National Review	"How Many Homeless?" September 25, 1987.
Newsweek	"Charity and Cynicism for the Homeless," November 14, 1988.
Robert Polner and Paul Schwartzman	"The Tragedy of Downward Mobility: Homelessness Hits the Middle Class," *In These Times,* September 28-October 4, 1988. Available from the Institute for Public Affairs, 1300 W. Belmont, Chicago, IL 60657.
Peter H. Rossi	"No Good Applied Social Research Goes Unpunished," *Society,* November/December 1987.
Nancy Rubin	"America's New Homeless," *McCall's,* November 1988.
USA Today	"Families of the Street," May 1987.
David Whitman	"Shattering Myths About the Homeless," *U.S. News & World Report,* March 20, 1989.

What Are the Causes of Homelessness?

Chapter Preface

Even though the homeless have been the subject of many studies, experts still disagree over why homelessness occurs. Two recent studies exemplify the diversity of opinion about this serious social problem.

In 1986, Richard B. Freeman and Brian Hall of Harvard University conducted an extensive study of homeless people in the United States. They found that 33 percent are mentally ill, 29 percent are alcoholics, and 14 percent are drug addicts. Freeman and Hall concluded that mental illness and addiction prevent these people from keeping jobs and integrating into society. Thus, they become homeless.

A very different conclusion was reached by Jonathan Kozol, author of *Rachel and Her Children*, his study of the homeless. Kozol interviewed dozens of people who lost their jobs, lost their homes to fire, or were otherwise forced into homelessness by economic catastrophe. He points out that between 1980 and 1988, company mergers, closings, and other factors caused two million industrial jobs to disappear each year. Kozol believes that this has much to do with the increase in homelessness.

Mental illness, chemical dependency, and economic misfortune are only a few of the possible explanations for homelessness. The viewpoints in the following chapter examine these and other causes.

"The chronically and severely mentally ill are not proficient at coping with the stresses of this world. Therefore, they are vulnerable to eviction."

Mental Illness Causes Homelessness

H. Richard Lamb and John A. Talbott

In 1983, the American Psychiatric Association created a task force to examine the causes of homelessness. The following viewpoint is a summary of the task force's findings. It was written by H. Richard Lamb, a professor in the department of psychiatry at the University of Southern California School of Medicine in Los Angeles, and John A. Talbott, a professor in the department of psychiatry at the University of Maryland School of Medicine in Baltimore. They conclude that the mentally ill have certain characteristics which make them particularly vulnerable to homelessness. Many are unable to handle normal tenant-landlord relations and are evicted. Others, searching for freedom, leave those who care for them, but on their own soon stop taking their medication and deteriorate. Most are unable to pull themselves out of the situation once they are homeless.

As you read, consider the following questions:

1. What do the authors believe was wrong with the deinstitutionalization movement?
2. What is the path to homelessness, according to Lamb and Talbott?

H. Richard Lamb and John A. Talbott, "The Homeless Mentally Ill: The Perspective of the American Psychiatric Assocation," *Journal of the American Medical Association*, vol. 256, no. 4, July 25, 1986, pp. 498-499. Copyright 1986, American Medical Assocation.

To see and experience the appalling conditions under which the homeless mentally ill exist has a profound impact on us; our natural reaction is a desire to rectify the horrors of what we see with a quick, bold stroke. But for the chronically mentally ill, homelessness is a complex problem with multiple causative factors. In our analysis of this problem, we must guard against settling for the simplistic explanations and solutions.

To address this problem, the American Psychiatric Association appointed a Task Force on the Homeless Mentally Ill in 1983, realizing that while all citizens have a responsibility for the welfare of the homeless, psychiatrists have an additional responsibility for the mentally ill among them. The recommendations of the Task Force have been adopted as official policy of the American Psychiatric Association.

One of the first decisions the Task Force had to make concerned the scope of the population to be addressed. While we all were concerned deeply about the homeless population in general, we believed that we needed to focus our efforts on those homeless persons who are chronically and severely mentally ill. The most methodologically sound studies performed thus far indicate that among the total population of homeless persons, there is a prevalence of about 40% with major mental illness (that is, schizophrenia and major affective disorder). Another way to define those homeless persons with whom we concerned ourselves were those who would have lived out their lives in state hospitals before deinstitutionalization. . . .

Poor Planning

We on the Task Force wanted to take an in-depth look at the underlying causes of homelessness, so that simplistic solutions would not be adopted hurriedly. We feared that in its haste to get the homeless mentally ill out of sight and out of mind, our society would resort to large-scale reinstitutionalization or an inappropriate reliance on shelters. The latter, while a necessary emergency resource, obviously do not constitute a long-term solution. We also wanted to forestall other naive and simplistic proposals—for instance, that such a complex problem as homelessness among the chronically and severely mentally ill could be solved simply by giving each member of this unfortunate group his or her own low-cost apartment in which to live alone.

We on the Task Force concluded that the concept of deinstitutionalization per se was not bad. The idea that many, if not most, of the severely and chronically mentally ill suffering from serious illnesses, such as schizophrenia and manic-depressive illness, could be cared for as well if not better in community programs as in institutions in itself was not a bad idea. It was clinically sound and economically feasible.

However, the way deinstitutionalization was originally carried out—through the poorly planned discharge of many thousands of mentally ill residents of state hospitals into inadequately prepared or programmatically deficient communities—was another thing altogether. In addition, as a result of the states' admission diversion policies, increasing numbers of "new" chronically mentally ill individuals have never been institutionalized and have further expanded the homeless mentally ill population.

Brain Diseases

I want to focus on the seriously mentally ill. I want to focus on them because they are the most disturbed group of the homeless population. They are also the most disturbing group. . . .

These people became homeless because we emptied out the state mental hospitals. . . .

We thought that all you had to do was empty the hospitals out, open up the gates, and they would live happily ever after. Well, if you drive around downtown Washington, you will see that they are not living happily ever after. These people have brain diseases. We now understand that the brain diseases are like multiple sclerosis and Alzheimer's disease. They are diseases of the body that affect the brain and, therefore, we have to do more than simply open up the doors and hope that they live happily ever after.

E. Fuller Torrey, *The Heritage Lectures: Rethinking Policy on Homelessness*, 1989.

Vital resources for both groups have been lacking. They include adequate and integrated community programs; an adequate number and range of community residential settings, with varying degrees of supervision and structure; a system of follow-up, monitoring, and responsibility for ensuring that services are provided to those unable to obtain them; and easy access to short- and long-term inpatient care when indicated. The consequences of these gaps in essential resources have been disastrous—one of these consequences was homelessness.

Becoming Homeless

How do the chronically mentally ill become homeless? Obviously, there are many pathways to the streets, but we think it is useful to look briefly at some of them. The chronically and severely mentally ill are not proficient at coping with the stresses of this world. Therefore, they are vulnerable to eviction from their living arrangements, sometimes because of an inability to deal with difficult or even ordinary landlord-tenant situations and sometimes because of circumstances in which they play a leading role. In the absence of an adequate case management system, they

57

are out on the streets and on their own. Many, especially the young, have a tendency to drift away from their families or from a board and care home; they may be trying to escape the pull of dependency and may not be ready to come to terms with living in a sheltered, low-pressure environment. If they still have goals, they may find an inactive life-style extremely depressing. Or they may want more freedom to drink or to use street drugs. Some may regard leaving their comparatively static milieu as a necessary part of the process of realizing their goals, but this is a process that exacts its price in terms of homelessness, crises, decompensation, and hospitalizations. Once the mentally ill are out on their own, they will more than likely stop taking their medications and after a while will lose touch with the Social Security Administration and will no longer be able to receive their Supplemental Security Income checks. Their poor judgment and the state of disarray associated with their illness may cause them to fail to notify the Social Security Administration of a change of address or to fail to appear for a redetermination hearing. Their lack of medical care on the streets and the effects of alcohol and other drug abuse are further serious complications. They may now be too disorganized to extricate themselves from living on the streets—except by exhibiting blatantly bizarre or disruptive behavior that leads to their being taken to a hospital or jail.

Victims of Naïveté

With the advantage of hindsight, we can see that the era of deinstitutionalization was ushered in with much naïveté and many simplistic notions about what would become of the chronically and severely mentally ill. The importance of psychoactive medication and a stable source of financial support was perceived, but the importance of developing such fundamental resources as supportive living arrangements was often not clearly seen or at least not implemented. "Community treatment" was much discussed, but there was no clear idea as to what it should consist of. The resistance of community mental health centers to providing services to the chronically mentally ill was not anticipated, nor was it foreseen how reluctant many states would be to allocate funds to community-based services.

In the midst of valid concerns about the shortcomings and antitherapeutic aspects of state hospitals, it was not appreciated that the state hospitals fulfilled some very crucial functions for the chronically and severely mentally ill. The term *asylum* was in many ways an appropriate one, for these imperfect institutions did provide asylum and sanctuary from the pressures of the world with which, in varying degrees, most of these patients were unable to cope. Further, these institutions provided such services as medical care, patient monitoring, respite for the patient's family,

Incidence of Mental Illness Among the Adult Sheltered Homeless by Region, 1984 and 1988

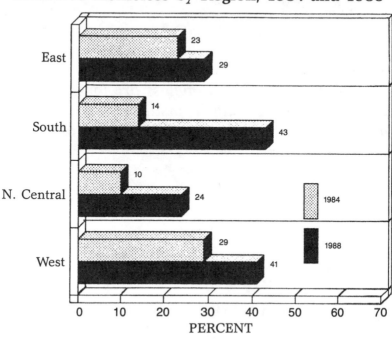

East
- 23
- 29

South
- 14
- 43

N. Central
- 10
- 24

West
- 29
- 41

1984
1988

0 10 20 30 40 50 60 70
PERCENT

U.S. Department of Housing and Urban Development, *The 1988 Survey of Shelters for the Homeless*, March 1989.

and a social network for the patient, as well as food and shelter and needed support and structure.

In the state hospitals, the treatment and services that did exist were in one place and under one administration. In the community, the situation is very different. Services and treatment are under various administrative jurisdictions and in various locations. Even the mentally healthy have difficulty dealing with a number of bureaucracies, both governmental and private, and getting their needs met. Further, patients can get lost easily in the community compared with a hospital—they may have been neglected, but at least their whereabouts were known. It is these problems that have led to the recognition of the importance of case management. It is probable that many of the homeless mentally ill would not be on the streets if they were on the caseload of a professional or paraprofessional case manager trained to deal with the problems of the chronically mentally ill, to monitor them (with considerable persistence when necessary), and to facilitate their receiving services.

"The notion that the homeless are largely psychotics who belong in institutions . . . spares us from the need to offer realistic solutions."

Mental Illness Does Not Cause Homelessness

Jonathan Kozol

Jonathan Kozol is the author of the much-acclaimed *Rachel and Her Children*, a book about homeless families living in the Martinique Hotel in New York City. In the following viewpoint, Kozol argues that the majority of homeless people are not mentally ill. The homeless may act depressed, bewildered, and angry, but these emotions are normal responses to the stressful and unpredictable lives they lead, he believes.

As you read, consider the following questions:

1. What is the real cause of homelessness, according to Kozol?
2. How does Kozol answer the argument that the deinstitutionalization of mental patients caused homelessness?
3. Why do the homeless often appear to be mentally ill, according to the author?

Jonathan Kozol, "Are the Homeless Crazy?" *Harper's Magazine*, September 1988. Reprinted with the author's permission.

It is commonly believed by many journalists and politicians that the homeless of America are, in large part, former patients of large mental hospitals who were deinstitutionalized in the 1970s—the consequence, it is sometimes said, of misguided liberal opinion that favored the treatment of such persons in community-based centers. It is argued that this policy, and the subsequent failure of society to build such centers or to provide them in sufficient number, is the primary cause of homelessness in the United States.

Those who work among the homeless do not find that explanation satisfactory. While conceding that a certain number of the homeless are or have been mentally unwell, they believe that, in the case of most unsheltered people, the primary reason is economic rather than clinical. The cause of homelessness, they say with disarming logic, is the lack of homes and of income with which to rent or acquire them.

They point to the loss of traditional jobs in industry (2 million every year since 1980) and to the fact that half of those who are laid off end up in work that pays a poverty-level wage. They point out that since 1968 the number of children living in poverty has grown by 3 million, while welfare benefits to families with children have declined by 35 percent.

And they note, too, that these developments have occurred during a time in which the shortage of low-income housing has intensified as the gentrification of our major cities has accelerated. Half a million units of low-income housing are lost each year to condominium conversion as well as to arson, demolition, or abandonment. Between 1978 and 1980, median rents climbed 30 percent for people in the lowest income sector, driving many of these families into the streets. Since 1980, rents have risen at even faster rates.

Stigmatizing Labels

Hard numbers, in this instance, would appear to be of greater help than psychiatric labels in telling us why so many people become homeless. Eight million American families now use half or more of their income to pay their rent or mortgage. At the same time, federal support for low-income housing dropped from $30 billion (1980) to $7.5 billion (1988). Under Presidents Ford and Carter, 500,000 subsidized private housing units were constructed. By President Reagan's second term, the number had dropped to 25,000.

In our rush to explain the homeless as a psychiatric problem even the words of medical practitioners who care for homeless people have been curiously ignored. A study published by the Massachusetts Medical Society, for instance, has noted that, with the exceptions of alcohol and drug use, the most frequent illnesses among a sample of the homeless population were trauma (31 percent), upper-respiratory disorders (28 percent), limb disorders (19 percent), mental illness (16 percent), skin diseases (15 percent), hypertension (14 percent), and neurological illnesses (12 percent). Why, we may ask, of all these calamities, does mental illness command so much political and press attention? The answer may be that the label of mental illness places the destitute outside the sphere of ordinary life. It personalizes an anguish that is public in its genesis; it individualizes a misery that is both general in cause and general in application.

There is another reason to assign labels to the destitute and single out mental illness from among their many afflictions. All these other problems—tuberculosis, asthma, scabies, diarrhea, bleeding gums, impacted teeth, etc.—bear no stigma, and mental illness does. It conveys a stigma in the United States. It conveys a stigma in the Soviet Union as well. In both nations the label is used, whether as a matter of deliberate policy or not, to isolate and treat as special cases those who, by deed or word or by sheer presence, represent a threat to national complacence. The two situations are obviously not identical, but they are enough alike to give Americans reason for concern.

Faulty Research

Some psychiatrists have maintained that most of the homeless are mentally ill and/or that their mental illness is the cause of the homelessness. These beliefs are largely the result of research studies with methodological weaknesses that have been conducted by psychiatrists and the mass media attention given to their flawed findings.

Richard H. Ropers, *The Invisible Homeless*, 1988.

The notion that the homeless are largely psychotics who belong in institutions, rather than victims of displacement at the hands of enterprising realtors, spares us from the need to offer realistic solutions to the deep and widening extremes of wealth and poverty in the United States. It also enables us to tell ourselves that the despair of homeless people bears no intimate connection to the privileged existence we enjoy—when, for example, we rent or purchase one of those restored town houses that once provided shelter for people now huddled in the street.

Loss of Housing

What is to be made, then, of the supposition that the homeless are primarily the former residents of mental hospitals, persons who were carelessly released during the 1970s? Many of them are, to be sure. Among the older men and women in the streets and shelters, as many as one-third (some believe as many as one-half) may be chronically disturbed, and a number of these people were deinstitutionalized during the 1970s. But to operate on that assumption in a city such as New York—where nearly half the homeless are small children whose average age is six—makes no sense. Their parents, with an average age of twenty-seven, are not likely to have been hospitalized in the 1970s, either.

A frequently cited set of figures tells us that in 1955 the average daily census of non-federal psychiatric institutions was 677,000, and that by 1984 the number had dropped to 151,000. But these people didn't go directly from a hospital room to the street. The bulk of those who had been psychiatric patients and were released from hospitals during the 1960s and early 1970s had been living in low-income housing, many in skid-row hotels or boardinghouses. Such housing—commonly known as SRO (single-room occupancy) units—was drastically diminished by the gentrification of our cities that began in the early '70s. Almost 50 percent of SRO housing was replaced by luxury apartments or office buildings between 1970 and 1980, and the remaining units have been disappearing even more rapidly.

Even for those persons who are ill and were deinstitutionalized during the decades before 1980, the precipitating cause of homelessness is not illness but loss of housing. SRO housing offered low-cost sanctuaries for the homeless, providing a degree of safety and mutual support for those who lived within them. They were a demeaning version of the community health centers that society had promised; they were the de facto "halfway houses" of the 1970s. For these people too—at most half of the homeless single persons in America—the cause of homelessness is lack of housing.

A Natural Response

Even in those cases where mental instability is apparent, homelessness itself is often the precipitating factor. For example, many pregnant women without homes are denied prenatal care because they constantly travel from one shelter to another. Many are anemic. Many are denied essential dietary supplements by federal cuts. As a consequence, some of their children do not live to see their second year of life. Do these mothers sometimes show signs of stress? Do they appear disorganized, depressed, disordered? Frequently. They are immobilized by pain, traumatized by fear. So it is no surprise that when researchers enter the scene to ask them how they "feel," the resulting reports tell us that the homeless are emotionally unwell. The reports do not tell us that we have *made* these people ill. They do not tell us that illness is a natural response to intolerable conditions. Nor do they tell us of the strength and the resilience that so many of these people retain despite the miseries they must endure.

A writer in the *New York Times* describes a homeless woman standing on a traffic island in Manhattan. "She was evicted from her small room in the hotel just across the street," and she is determined to get revenge. Until she does, "nothing will move her from that spot. . . . Her argumentativeness and her angry fixation on revenge, along with the apparent absence of hallucinations, mark her as paranoid." Most physicans, I imagine, would be more reserved in passing judgment with so little evidence, but this reporter makes his diagnosis without hesitation. "The paranoids of the street," he says, "are among the most difficult to help."

Screaming for Revenge

Perhaps so. But does it depend on who is offering the help? Is anyone offering to help this woman get back her home? Is it crazy to seek vengeance for being thrown into the street? The absence of anger, some psychiatrists believe, might indicate much greater illness.

An Unfortunate Belief

Although only one-third of homeless people nationwide are mentally disabled, since the early 1980s homelessness has become synonymous in the public mind with mental illness. What we have done, then, is taken one stigmatized illness, alcoholism, and replaced it with another, mental illness, as a stereotype for the homeless. People may assume that most or all homeless people are mentally ill, partly because like that of the alcoholic, the lifestyle of the mentally ill homeless person is visible to the general public. A friend of mine who is a businessman in Phoenix, when discussing the location of a shelter for the homeless, said to me, "I think it should be on the grounds of the state hospital." When I gasped, he said, "Now look, you know and I know that anybody who is on the street has to be mentally ill." Unfortunately, that is the perception of many people.

Louisa Stark, *Homelessness: Critical Issues for Policy and Practice*, 1987.

"No one will be turned away," says the mayor of New York City, as hundreds of young mothers with their infants are turned from the doors of shelters season after season. That may sound to some like a denial of reality. . . .

The woman standing on the traffic island screaming for revenge until her room has been restored to her sounds relatively healthy by comparison. If 3 million homeless people did the same, and all at the same time, we might finally be forced to listen.

Lack of Affordable Housing Causes Homelessness

James D. Wright and Julie A. Lam

James D. Wright is director of research and Julie A. Lam is a research assistant at the Social and Demographic Research Institute of the University of Massachusetts in Boston. In the following viewpoint, Wright and Lam argue that the lack of affordable housing is the major cause of homelessness. Mental illness, drug addiction, and other often-mentioned causes are of less importance, they contend, since even if these factors could be eliminated there would still be people who could not afford housing. They argue that low-cost housing has been demolished at the same time as increasing numbers of Americans have slipped below the poverty line, making housing costs out of reach for many.

As you read, consider the following questions:

1. What two trends do the authors believe have made housing less affordable?
2. What caused an overall shortage of rental housing, according to Wright and Lam?
3. Why do the authors argue that current methods of helping the homeless are inadequate?

James D. Wright and Julie A. Lam, "Homelessness and the Low-Income Housing Supply," *Social Policy*, Spring 1987. Reprinted by permission of SOCIAL POLICY, published by Social Policy Corporation, New York, NY 10036. Copyright 1987 by Social Policy Corporation.

In the first line of analysis, *homelessness is a housing problem*. This perhaps seems too obvious to mention (much less to serve as a major theme), except that much that has been written about homelessness makes reference to the housing problem only in passing, the more basic focus being on problems of unemployment, or on deinstitutionalization and attendant issues of mental health, or on alcohol and other substance abuse, or on the cutbacks in social welfare spending by the Reagan Administration. All of these, to be sure, are important factors; viewed structually, however, the trends discussed here in the poverty housing supply and the poverty population conspire to create a housing "game" that increasing numbers are destined to lose. Much of the literature is focused on who the "losers" are; our interest here is in the nature of the game itself.

That housing in the United States has become generally more expensive in recent decades will come as no surprise. The average price of single-family dwellings sold in 1970 was $23,000; in 1980, the figure was $62,200, and in 1983, $70,300. More to the present point, the median gross monthly rent for renter-occupied units has shown an equivalent trend: In 1970, the median monthly rent was $108; in 1980, $243; and in 1983, $315. In most cities, of course, low-income housing consists almost exclusively of rental units.

The general effect of inflation on the supply of low-income rental housing is illustrated by the trend in the total number of units nationwide renting for $80 or less per month. In 1970, these units numbered some 5.5 million; in 1980, 1.1 million; and in 1983, 650,000. A family who could afford to spend no more than $80 per month on rent would, therefore, have seen its supply of potential housing cut nearly in half in the brief span of three years, and cut by nearly 90 percent over the longer term.

Sinking into Poverty

A second large-scale trend, not quite so well known as the first, is the recent increase in the percentage of U.S. citizens living at or below the poverty level. This percentage exceeded 20 percent up through the early 1960s, but had fallen to 12.6 percent by 1970. The rate hovered between 12.6 percent and 11.1 percent throughout the 1970s, with no obvious trend in either direction. Beginning in 1980, the poverty percentage started to climb. The 1980 figure, 13.0 percent, was the highest figure recorded since 1969, and the poverty rate has continued to climb since—to 15.2 percent in 1983.

The period between 1980 and 1983 is of particular interest because it spans the emergence of public concern over the problem of homelessness. The rather sudden rise of concern can be indexed by the number of listings under "homelessness" in the *Reader's*

Guide to Periodical Literature. In 1980, there were no listings. In 1981, there were 3 listings; in 1982, 15; in 1983, 21, and in 1984, 32. Clearly, during the early years of the 1980s, homelessness became a "hot topic."

Based on the evidence so far reviewed, this emerging concern over the problem is understandable. Indeed, it is a reasonable inference from these data that never before in postwar American history have so many poor people competed for so few affordable dwelling units. In itself, this is not news; much has been written in the past decade about the low-income housing crisis, especially in the big cities. What has not yet been discussed in adequate detail is the apparent connection between this housing crisis and the rise of the homelessness problem. The "new homeless," we suggest, are best conceptualized as the losers in this increasingly unfavorable housing competition. . . .

Between the late 1970s and the early 1980s, the poverty population increased sharply, while the supply of low-income housing dwindled just as sharply. At virtually the same time, the *visibility*

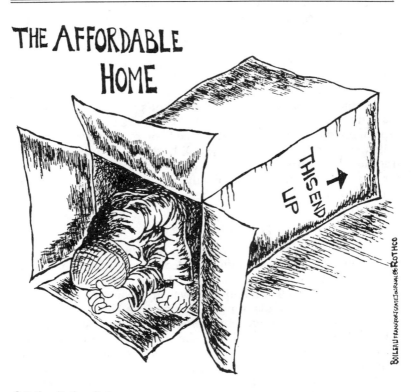

© Boileau/Rothco Cartoons

of the homelessness problem increased, as did the amount of attention devoted to the problem. It is hard to imagine that this is sheer coincidence.

Destroying Affordable Housing

What accounts for the sudden and dramatic loss of low-income housing in the large cities? It is obvious that the general rate of inflation in consumer prices for all commodities is a major villain, but it is not the whole story. Inflation will increase the price that must be paid for a particular housing unit, but at least the unit is still *there*. Not so the units bulldozed to the ground to make way for urban renewal or for the revitalization of "downtown." What we have witnessed in the past few years is not just an increase in the average price of rental housing, but an absolute loss of low-income units through outright destruction or through conversion to other, more profitable uses.

Between 1974 and 1979, the net loss (units created less units withdrawn) averaged some 360,000 rental units *annually*. "Nowhere near enough rental units were being constructed to replace those withdrawn from use," [according to Anthony Downs]. Chester Hartman, in the same vein, has noted "the decreasing supply of rental housing because of inadequate construction levels, conversion of apartments to condominiums, and abandonment of rental units." Most observers would agree that the lost rental units have been drawn very disproportionately from the low-income housing stock.

National data on the types of rental units being decimated apparently do not exist. There is a small literature on one particular type of low-income unit bearing directly on our concerns: the so-called single-room occupancy (SRO) boarding houses that have traditionally figured prominently as the "housing of last resort" for the socially and economically marginal population. The elimination of SRO housing has been called "a widespread trend across the country.". . .

The New Homeless

The SROs and low-income rental housing in general have suffered considerably in the much-lauded effort to "revitalize the cities." A national study of the phenomenon shows that, overall, some 5 percent of all residential moves in urban areas represent forced relocation, that is, unwanted displacement. According to one calculation, this represents some 2.5 million displaced persons *each year*. Characteristics of the residentially displaced include high housing-cost burdens (rents as a fraction of income), central-city residence, being on welfare, and low levels of educational achievement. "The analysis produced a consistent picture of lower-income families being most susceptible to displacement," [according to Sandra Newman and Michael S. Owen]. . . .

In the 1960s and even in the early 1970s, families displaced by these "revitalization" processes would often be relocated, for better or worse, in publicly-subsidized low-income housing projects. In the late 1970s and especially in the 1980s, however, the federal government drastically reduced its subsidies for the construction of low-income housing. Today, there is virtually no low-income housing being built anywhere, and yet the demand and the need for such housing is, if anything, increasing. What, then, becomes of the displaced now that public housing is no longer a viable alternative? If the analysis reported here is even approximately correct, then some of the displaced—no doubt, the most vulnerable among them—remain more or less permanently displaced, and these, we suggest, have come to be known as the "new homeless."

A Housing Catastrophe

It was possible to write, as early as 1972, that "the United States is in the midst of a severe housing crisis." In the years since, the urban housing situation has changed from critical to catastrophic. The increase in the urban poverty population, coupled with a sharp reduction in the amount of available low-income housing, have conspired to create a new class of urban homeless. Arising in tandem with the emergence of this class is a new tier of social service agencies, advocates, social workers, and others to minister to the human suffering that has resulted.

Evidence of the Shortage

The primary cause of homelessness is an inadequate supply of housing, especially at the bottom of the rental market. And government policy is deeply implicated.

Evidence for the shortage of low income housing abounds. Vacancy rates in New York, San Francisco, and Boston have averaged 1 to 2 percent (5 percent is considered normal). Homelessness is only the most visible component of the undersupply problem. In New York City, more than 300,000 people are doubled up with friends and relatives.

Todd Swanstrom, *The New York Times*, March 23, 1989.

"What to do about homelessness?" is a question that now commands considerable attention among researchers, advocates, and social policy-makers. Most of the answers that have so far been provided are ameliorative in character: the homeless need more and better shelters, food, community mental health services, alcohol education and counselling, medical care, job counselling and placement, and on through the list of basic human needs. All of these, to be sure, are genuine needs, and the effort to respond to them is compassionate and laudable. But, in the first instance, the homeless need housing, and nothing short of providing more low-income housing will solve the homelessness problem.

The point, it appears, is not lost on the homeless themselves. In a report, based on a "needs assessment" survey of 112 homeless people in the San Francisco area, respondents were asked to identify "the most important issues you face or problems you have trying to make it in San Francisco or generally in life." "No place to live indoors" was the most common response, mentioned by 94 percent; "no money" was second, mentioned by 88 percent. These were the only responses mentioned by at least half the sample.

Victims of the Economy

Every study yet done of the homeless has reported a range of social and personal pathologies. Depending upon sample, definitions, and the professional interests of the investigators, somewhere between 29 and 55 percent of the homeless are reported to have a serious drinking problem, somewhere between 10 and 30 percent are reported to have a problem with other substance dependencies, and somewhere between 20 and 84 percent are reported to be emotionally disturbed or mentally ill. Other common problems include prior criminal records, a history of psychiatric hospitalization, physical or sexual abuse as children, and profound estrangement from family and friends.

In some sense, of course, these factors are appropriately cited as the "cause" of a person's homelessness, just as consistent bad luck can be cited as the "cause" of losing at cards. Given a game that some are destined to lose, it is appropriate to do research on who the losers turn out to be. But we should not mistake an analysis of the losers for an analysis of the game itself. The data reported here suggest that in a hypothetical world where there are no alcoholics, no drug addicts, no mentally ill, no deinstitutionalization movement, indeed, no personal or social pathologies at all, there would still be a formidable homelessness problem, simply because at this stage in American history, there is not enough low-income housing to accommodate the poverty population. The new homeless, we suggest, are to be seen largely as victims of a housing economy that is, assuredly, not of their own making.

"The most important element in the explosive growth of homelessness . . . [is] the sudden devaluation of the family in America."

Family Breakdown Causes Homelessness

Dan McMurry

Dan McMurry is an associate professor of sociology at Middle Tennessee State University at Murfreesboro. To find out more about the homeless, McMurry posed as a street person and wandered across the country. What he discovered was that most of the homeless did not have strong ties with their families. Divorce, he argues, has left many of the poor without a family to help them when their money is depleted. Weakened ties have meant that people no longer feel that they must take care of their own relatives, according to McMurry.

As you read, consider the following questions:

1. How has the homeless population changed, in the author's opinion?
2. What are the differences between the effects of divorce on the poor and the effects on the middle class, according to the author?
3. What does McMurry contend is the relationship between drug addiction and homelessness?

Dan McMurry, "Down and Out in America," *Crisis*, February 1989. Reprinted with permission of *Crisis* magazine, PO Box 1006, Notre Dame, IN 46556.

For a few years in the early 1980s, I spent part of each summer at the University of California at Berkeley. I always stayed in San Francisco and rode the subway back and forth. It was there, in 1983, that I first discovered street people. The streets were full of them, crying "spare change, Mister?" and lying in doorways and alleys. They were a real puzzle to me because until then I thought I understood the homeless.

I had been looking at homeless transients for a long time as part of my professional concern. In the early 1970s, I began teaching a course at Middle Tennessee State University on the sociology of alcohol, and as part of the course I often took the students to the Nashville Union Rescue Mission to see the situation firsthand and to hear Reverend Carl Resener lecture on alcoholism. Until about 1980, I could predict who would be at the mission and what kind of people they would be. Any careful observer could.

Then things changed—and quickly. The numbers of the homeless exploded and women and children, totally absent until now, were seen from time to time. They spilled over the boundaries of the old Skid Rows and out of the missions onto the streets and into the parks. And, exceedingly important, a group of people who were virtually ignored by the media suddenly became the darlings of the press.

The media now presented a problem. Since I had been studying the residents of the streets for years and was closely watching the changing scene, newspaper articles and TV specials on the homeless did not ring true. University students who have a special need for unadorned, factual information (for they will make the next cycle of decisions about our social world) were being partly informed and sadly misinformed.

Joining the Ranks

In order to study the situation from a firsthand vantage point, I began posing as a street person. First, in San Francisco on the sly, then over Christmas vacations in Texas and Tennessee, until finally I had the nerve to do it officially with the support and blessing of the university. The support and blessing of Carolyn, my wife, was much more difficult to obtain, and even then was offered a bit grudgingly. Our domestic tranquility was fractured by her reaction to my statement, "Hey, Hon, I think I'll go down to Nashville and lie around on the streets for a few days. Sorry I can't be at your Christmas party."

I stopped shaving and let my hair and beard grow again. Beginning in spring 1988, I roamed from Charlotte to Richmond to Washington to New York to Chicago to Omaha to Denver to Cheyenne to Billings to Salt Lake City to Las Vegas to Los Angeles and back, posing as a street person. . . .

Let me tell you what I have learned. . . .

A small, but rapidly growing group of researchers and observers have identified as the most important element in the explosive growth of homelessness the change in the cohesiveness of the American family. More precisely, the change has been the sudden devaluation of the family in America. Divorce and the increasing unpopularity of marriage have wreaked havoc among the poor.

A Common Pattern

While there is no uniform profile for homeless families, our research uncovered patterns common to many. The majority of women had lived in unstable situations before coming to the shelter. The sheltering facilities were just brief stops in patterns of instability and family disruption.

Ellen L. Bassuk, Alison S. Lauriat, and Leonore Rubin, *Homelessness: Critical Issues for Policy and Practice*, 1987.

Most studies fail to recognize the impact of family dissolution on homelessness. Divorce adds a far heavier burden to poor families than it does to families at the social level from which those who conduct the studies come. It is difficult for middle-class observers to recognize, to say nothing of to understand, the impact that the disruption of family ties has had upon the poor during the past two decades.

The results of divorce among the affluent is perhaps ulcer-producing stress, a little rumor around the office, and great concern for the impact on career and finances. (We may receive a few disturbing, late night phone calls from some of our many friends who are experiencing the trauma.) But to assume that these are the effects of divorce on poor families is to misunderstand completely how vital families are, and have always been, to the poor.

Pathetic Consequences

This surge of divorce has produced among poor Americans a dissolution of family structure having pathetic consequences far beyond our middle-class comprehension. For these people, family and friends have always meant, not camaraderie and companionship, but survival. These are the ties that bind. Families cling together for the same reason soldiers cleave together and small children hold hands in the dark. But many poor families no longer feel required, or even *expected*, to care for their own when the situation involves sacrifice or commitment.

A case involving one of the friends I made on the streets clearly shows the impact of ruptured family bonds. His name was John. I met him on the steps of a mission. His face was severely beaten. He needed help. I bummed a cigarette for him. He was from a small town in Georgia. I took him to Traveler's Aid, and they said they would gladly buy him a bus ticket home if he would give them the telephone number of someone who would say he had a place to come home to. He said he would come back later with the number. Once outside, he told me that we would have to find another way to help him. I asked why. He said he could not furnish them with a telephone number. He said that he had a current wife, two ex-wives, a mother, a stepfather, an uncle, and three married children, but none of them would say "yes" to the Traveler's Aid question.

One morning in Gallatin, I talked with a shelter director preparing to meet that afternoon with two sisters, aged 19 and 21, who between them had five children and no husbands and were being kicked out of the house by their mother, who also had no husband. "What am I to do?" he asked me. "What I can do is try to adjust things to keep them there, or put them up in a motel for a few nights, but then they would drift from there to the streets." In the silence that followed, we both knew that whatever he did wouldn't fix what was broken. . . .

A Necessary Factor

The problems of the homeless are almost always a tangle of personal pathologies combined with fractured relationships. In one of the best empirical studies of the homeless it was discovered that about eight of ten had experienced some form of institutionalization for either drugs, mental problems, or crime. It is almost never alcoholism alone, or mental illness alone, that produces homelessness. Likewise, it is not poverty alone. Those of us born during the Depression know that. And in most cases, alcoholism combined with poverty, or mental disadvantage combined with alcoholism are not enough to land the unfortunate out on the street. The proximate cause of homelessness, and what accounts most for the explosion in their numbers, then, is fractured relationships.

"It is grossly naive to believe that alcohol has not contributed to the arrival of many of these men on skid row."

Alcoholism Contributes to Homelessness

Carl I. Cohen and Jay Sokolovsky

The Bowery is an infamous section of New York City known for its skid row hotels and homeless population. Its inhabitants were studied by Carl I. Cohen, of the State University of New York Health Science Center in Brooklyn, and Jay Sokolovsky, of the University of Maryland in Baltimore County. In the following viewpoint, Cohen and Sokolovsky contend that alcohol placed stress on the homeless men's family ties, consumed their money, and made them less productive workers. Cohen and Sokolovsky argue that without families to take the men in or jobs to support themselves, these men soon became homeless.

As you read, consider the following questions:

1. How prevalent is the use of alcohol among homeless men, according to the authors?
2. Why did many of the men Cohen and Sokolovsky surveyed begin drinking?
3. What characteristics did the heaviest drinkers in the authors' study show?

Carl I. Cohen and Jay Sokolovsky, *Old Men of the Bowery: Strategies for Survival Among the Homeless.* New York: The Guilford Press, 1989. Reprinted with permission of the authors and publisher.

When we began this project in 1982, we weren't sure whether the dramatic rise in homelessness might be a transient phenomenon, a glitch in the system. Perhaps with a little recalibration, the problem would disappear. By 1988, shelters were firmly embedded in the urban landscape. . . . Homelessness continues to worsen. A report released in December 1987 by the United States Conference of Mayors found that the demand for emergency food and shelter increased by approximately 20% nationwide over the previous year. In some cities the demand increased by more than twice this national average. Moreover, the percentage of homeless families grew by greater than one-third.

The litany of statistics and outrage, however, has been undermined by a generalized psychic numbing. Along with cold steel fireplugs and ruptured garbage bags, the homeless person has become just one more object on the sidewalk. Newspapers and T.V. now spew forth a daily dose of homeless stories along with the murders, fires, weather, and sports. And subtly, there has been a shift in parlance from "Homelessness"—suggesting a social origin—to "The Homeless Problem," which implies that the cause may be within the homeless person. . . .

In this work our aim is to refocus the debate. Previous studies of the homeless have tended to be either too system-oriented or too individual-oriented. We have addressed both levels—the personal casualties as well as the systemic causalities. We have combined anthropological, psychological, and sociological methods and have drawn upon the lives of older homeless men not to consign individual blame, but to illuminate the interplay of biography and society. Their life pathways point to where today's young homeless will head if meaningful interventions are not introduced. . . .

The Role of Alcohol

Until recently, the general public believed that alcoholism was synonymous with skid row. This misconception did a disservice to two populations: (1) those alcoholics in the general population who were rarely identified as such by family and friends because they thought alcoholics must be skid row types; (2) skid rowers who were seen as deserving of their destitution because of their debauchery. On the other hand, it is grossly naive to believe that alcohol has not contributed to the arrival of many of these men on skid row, their continued existence on skid row, and their physical and mental deterioration. To date, however, the literature has been equivocal as to what extent alcohol explains and maintains homelessness and skid row existence.

Nels Anderson's (1923) early work done during the height of Prohibition noted that "drinking is responsible for keeping many men on the road." Anderson further observed, "Practically all homeless men drink when liquor is available. The only sober moments for many hobos and tramps are when they are without funds." The study by E.H. Sutherland and H.J. Locke (1936) of Chicago's Shelter population in the 1930s suggested that alcohol was both a "cause and effect in a process of interacting factors." Excessive alcohol intake often resulted in marital breakup, loss of job, and eventual decline to homelessness. Correspondingly, many men, after a loss of job or marital difficulty, turned to alcohol for solace. Donald Bogue's (1963) study of Chicago's skid row in the 1950s indicated that among the heaviest drinkers (32% of his sample), four fifths of the men had started their uncontrolled drinking before their 35th birthday. Thus, based on Bogue's data, a majority of these men were already drinking heavily prior to coming to skid row. Similarly, Robert Strauss's 1946 study of 203 homeless men reported heavy use of alcohol among 80% to 85% of the men and that two thirds had begun drinking prior to becoming homeless. Strauss, however, cautioned that alcoholism was one of many contributing factors leading to homelessness and that alcohol might be a way for homeless men to adjust to the world. In other words, although heavy drinking often starts prior to entry to skid row, for many men (at least one third) heavy drinking may begin after beginning a skid row life. . . .

Still Heavy Drinkers

All studies of the old homeless stress the widespread prevalence of chronic alcoholism, and here the new homeless are little different. Donald Bogue found that 30 percent of his sample were heavy drinkers, defined as persons spending 25 percent or more of their income on alcohol and drinking the equivalent of six or more pints of whiskey a week. Using comparable measures, Howard Bahr and Theodore Caplow found 36 percent to be heavy drinkers. Similar proportions were found in Minneapolis and Philadelphia.

Peter H. Rossi, *Without Shelter,* 1989.

It would seem from the literature that the pendulum has swung to the point that skid rowers and homeless men are no longer viewed as alcoholics. . . . Nevertheless, our data suggest that these assumptions require some modification, especially among older skid row men. First, alcohol use was widespread and consumption was substantial. Fewer than 2% of the men claimed that they never drank alcohol and 80% reported that they still drink. By their own estimates (which are certainly conservative), 21%, 22%, and 20% of the men reported that they are moderate, heavy, or spree drinkers, respectively; 49% of the men drink daily, and another 33% drink several times per week. Drinking among the street men was exceptionally high, 90% of the men were either moderate, heavy, or spree drinkers; 37% classified themselves as "heavy" consumers. We found that 58% of the street men drank daily, and 36% drank several times a week.

Men who drank only wine comprised 16% of our sample, while 25% drank only beer, 19% drank only hard liquor, and 41% drank a combination of alcoholic beverages (usually wine and something else) or as several men put it, "whatever is available.". . .

Alcohol has played a powerful role in these men's lives. Nearly one fifth of the men listed alcohol specifically as a primary or secondary reason for coming to the Bowery, although it also contributed indirectly through impoverishment (the major reason most men came) and family problems. These men had been drinking moderately or heavily on the average of nine years prior to coming to the Bowery. This is consistent with the early studies of Robert Strauss (1946) who found that two thirds of homeless men had begun their heavy drinking prior to arrival on skid row.

For many men, drinking began early and created a lifetime of instability. For example, Uncle Ed first began drinking as a teenager when he ran away from home and ended up in Newark. There, he started hanging around with the "bottle boys." As he put it, "What started me drinkin'? Just kind of hangin' around with the guys. What the hell, they're drinkin'. I'll drink too. That's all. No real reason. Just to be one of the boys."

A Way to Belong

Several of the men who started early in life echoed Ed's sentiments. Alcohol was a way to belong, of becoming part of the group:

> I started drinkin' at 15 but it wasn't nothin' serious 'cause I was goin' to school at that time and I drank only on Saturday. I never really knew why I drank. I used to like it at first when I was a kid. I started as a lark. I still don't know why I drink now. I don't like it. I really don't.

A number of the early onset drinkers began imbibing heavily because drinking was a common pastime among their fellow-workers. Ed, while working as a dishwasher in Boston, used to go out drinking with his co-workers on the weekend. Also, beer was usually passed around when the men were working the night shift. Miles also began drinking heavily after losing his steady job and had to accept seasonal jobs working in the kitchens of the Catskill hotels. Most of the kitchen men drank heavily. Miles viewed alcohol as medicinal: "You know I need it. It calms my nerves." Other men claimed to have begun their heavy consumption after their marriage broke up or after a family death or tragedy:

Incidence of Alcoholism Among the Adult Sheltered Homeless by Region, 1984 and 1988

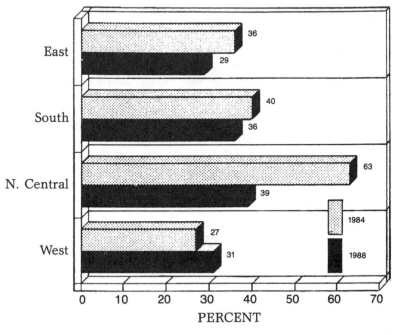

U.S. Department of Housing and Urban Development, *The 1988 Survey of Shelters for the Homeless*, March 1989.

Mr. Rodriguez lost his entire family, uncles, aunts, parents, grandparents, and so forth in a flood in Texas in 1957. He then started falling apart, and in 1961 he said he became a full fledged alcoholic. He drank extremely heavily for four years during which time he said he was hospitalized from "300 to 400" times (unbelievable?!) for alcoholism. He was finally put in intensive care a couple of times and from that scare or shock, quit drinking and thereafter started smoking a lot of pot. He smoked up most of his earnings and has recently quit that. . . .

The price that alcohol has exacted on their families and in missed employment opportunities is legion:

Mr. Davis blames his situation on the booze. He sees patterns in what he does and really wants to get it together before it's too late. He has a summer job in the mountains and wishes not to return to the Bowery. Most of his life he worked as a tractor-trailer driver. He sees rigs drive by, looks at the driver and says to himself "Now why aren't I still doing that." Then he says, "I think the quart of booze per day took its toll."

Mr. George was forced to leave home after separating from his wife. He attributes most of his problems to alcohol abuse. He seems fairly isolated living on the Bowery and often spoke about his wife and relatives who live in Mount Vernon, N.Y. He is unhappy about the infrequent contact he has with them.

As noted previously, many of the men had symptoms associated with alcohol abuse: 12% had seizure disorders, 37% were tremulous, 45% had dizziness, 16% had visual hallucinations, and 28% had incurred fractures in the past ten years. We developed a scale comprised of 3 items: age of onset of heavy drinking (before age 35), quantity, and frequency of alcohol consumption. The alcohol scale was found to have a weak but significant relationship with poor physical health, failure to fulfill material needs, increased social interaction, depression, and an inverse relationship to age. In other words, within our sample, those who drank the most tended to be younger, in poorer physical health, more depressed, and less capable of meeting their daily needs. . . .

A Key Role

Alcohol plays a key role in the formation of the Bowery man. We found that moderate and heavy alcohol consumption preceded by nearly a decade a man's permanent arrival on the Bowery. Here, it is possible to see how several factors can potentiate each other. Marginal poverty and periodic unemployment create personal and family stressors which in turn produce increased exposure and desire for alcohol; increased alcohol consumption makes it more difficult to hold a job, as well as further exacerbating family strain. Upton Sinclair (1905) graphically describes this battle:

> One day, however, he took the plunge, and drank up all that he had in his pockets, and went home half "piped," as the men phrase it. He was happier than he had been in a year; and yet, because he knew that the happiness would not last, he was savage, too—with those who would wreck it, and with the world, and with his life; and then again, beneath this, he was sick with the shame of himself. Afterward, when he saw the despair of his family, and reckoned up the money he had spent, the tears came into his eyes, and he began the long battle with the specter.

Nearly one in five men listed alcohol as their primary or secondary reason for coming to the Bowery, although alcohol was implicit in other reasons such as economics, family problems, or feeling comfortable on the Bowery.

In closing, it is important to note that not every person who is an alcoholic becomes homeless. Rather, alcoholism typically interacts with one or more other factors: a family history of poverty or near-poverty, vocational backgrounds in unskilled or semi-skilled labor, physical or mental impairments, and a social system that provides insufficient low-cost housing and few opportunities for these persons to earn adequate wages.

"Changes in the economy have deprived many people of the income with which to pay for housing."

Economic Factors Cause Homelessness

Peter Marcuse

In the following viewpoint, Peter Marcuse argues that the structure of the U.S. economy makes homelessness inevitable. He contends that housing is provided for workers when they are necessary to the economy. But when the economy changes, such as the switch from industrial to service sector jobs, excess workers are allowed to become homeless. Marcuse is a professor of urban planning at Columbia University in New York City.

As you read, consider the following questions:

1. What delayed the increase in the numbers of homeless, according to Marcuse?
2. What factors does the author believe ensured that housing was provided for the poor in the past?
3. Why do service jobs pay less than manufacturing jobs, in Marcuse's opinion?

Peter Marcuse, "Neutralizing Homelessness," *Socialist Review,* January 1988. Reprinted with permission of *Socialist Review.*

> They have always been with us. The same beggar who
> stretched a suppliant palm toward the passing togas of ancient
> Rome can be found today on Colfax Avenue in Denver, still
> thirsty for wine; the bruised and broken woman who slept in
> the gutters of medieval Paris now beds down in a cardboard box
> in a vest-pocket park in New York City.

This *Newsweek* quotation is profoundly wrong, if simplistically
right. Simplistically, past history has indeed consisted of class
societies, in which some have always been exploited by others
and the needs of those at the bottom have never been fully met.
But it is profoundly wrong to equate the situation today with that
of past years. Such comparisons conceal the specific nature and
causes of—and necessary remedies for—homelessness today.
However, the historical inaccuracy in the above quotation is no
accident. Rather, it represents a conscious ideological effort by
the dominant culture to neutralize the political implications of
homelessness, the shock of homelessness. . . .

Sweeping Away the Problem

Ignoring the problem, or concealing it, would be the easy way
out. Indeed, the George Wills of this world would simply sweep
it away:

> "If it is illegal . . . to litter the streets, frankly it ought to be
> illegal for people . . . to sleep in the streets. Therefore, there is
> a simple matter of public order and hygiene in getting these peo-
> ple somewhere else. Not arrest them, but move them off
> somewhere where they are simply out of sight. . . ."

But homelessness cannot be "moved off somewhere;" it is all
around us. It must be dealt with explicitly, neutralized. But to move
towards a permanent solution to the problem would require addressing its root causes, and thus would necessitate a virtual
revolution in public policy. It would require the acknowledgment
of the failure of the market to solve the housing problem, the provision of housing for all those in need, the care of those who are
outside the system. Yet such a "revolutionary" solution challenges
the fundamental economic, social and political fabric of US
society. . . .

The simplest definition of homelessness is "not having shelter
for the night." But that definition is hardly exhaustive: it leaves
open what shelter is—a roof over one's head? protection from the
elements? temporary shelter? And there are social attributes of
housing involved—is a person in a public emergency shelter not
homeless? Or one in a hospital, about to be discharged with no
place to go? Or a family living three to a room? These questions
can only be answered historically, not absolutely.

The major historical patterns of homelessness might be
separated out as follows:

A non-industrial pattern, in which the resources to provide all persons with minimally adequate housing are missing. The extent of homelessness is determined by the combination of absolute shortage and maldistribution of resources.

A pattern during early industrialization, in which the growing demand for workers in factories led to migration to cities in excess of the housing supply available for the migrants (or at prices not affordable with the wages being paid, which is the same thing). In this incarnation, homelessness is "rolling," rather than constant for any particular individuals; people migrate to the city and become temporarily homeless until more housing is built or they find lodgings. London and Paris at the end of the 18th and beginning of the 19th century are examples of this pattern.

A pattern under colonial exploitation, in which the impact of subordination in an international economic and political system, combined with a distorted form of "early" industrialization, produce a skewing of population and of resources that, superimposed upon resource scarcity, creates the phenomena we now see in many of the third world's giant cities. This pattern of homelessness is permanent and endemic, and in most cases escalating.

The pattern of mature industrialization within a private market economy, in which there is an unstable balance between the

number of low paid workers and unemployed, and the number of housing units available to them. The extent of homelessness here will be cyclical, in general paralleling fluctuations in the levels of employment and wages in the private economy.

The new pattern of deindustrialization prevailing in many contemporary industrialized private market economies such as the US, involving declines in manufacturing jobs, increases in the services sector, a heightened international division of labor, a "return to the city," all with the consequences for homelessness discussed below.

It is this last pattern of homelessness which characterizes the current phase of homelessness in the United States and differentiates it from other historical patterns of homelessness. Both the number of the homeless and the nature of homelessness changed significantly in the United States in the last twenty years. The magnitude of homelessness has changed drastically. The number of homeless in New York City, for example, has tripled between 1982 and 1986, and increased by 42 percent between 1986 and 1988. Kim Hopper and Jill Hamberg, in their pioneering study of the history of homelessness, speak of the crossing of an "invisible threshold"—the beginning of the new and rapid escalation of homelessness which most observers situate at about 1979. While the major economic transformations the term "deindustrialization" somewhat imprecisely describes were already well in place before then, general economic growth and political resistance had prevented the manifestation of numbers of homeless until this point. . . .

Causes of Homelessness

Homelessness has three related causes: the profit structure of housing, the distribution of income, and government policy. Briefly, housing is supplied for profit, as a commodity. There is no profit in supplying housing for those now homeless. The cost of provision has increased, and alternate uses are more profitable. Changes in the economy have deprived many people of the income with which to pay for housing. The government only acts to provide housing for persons unable to pay the market price when the economy may need such people in the future or when those people threaten the status quo. Neither situation prevails today. . . .

The structure of production is ultimately at the root both of what happens in the housing market and government policy. The influence is not always direct, it may in some cases not be decisive, but it is always present. The logic is straightforward: what the homeless get depends on what the poor get; what the poor get depends on how useful they are to the system, and how they deal with their position in it. When there is a shortage of labor, the poor are needed. Their housing is of concern, and very few end

84

up homeless, as was the situation during World War II, and during the post-War boom. When the poor are militant and the establishment is concerned about their possible actions, the homeless cannot be rejected or isolated. Even if they are not well housed, the government will make efforts to at least acknowledge housing of the poor as a public responsibility, as was the case in the Great Depression. But when there is a surplus of labor and the poor seem quiescent, the poor are not served, and the homeless bear the brunt. So it is today.

Rapid Changes

There are multiple causes for homelessness and persistent poverty in this country. Rapid changes in the economy account for much of the uprootedness. As the U.S. economy changes very rapidly to a world economy, corporations find and take opportunities to move manufacturing facilities outside the U.S. . . . Plants close without notice. Mass layoffs, production slowdowns, corporate buy-outs, and product changes are all considered management decisions, in spite of the fact that they can have devastating effects on the lives of the workers and their families.

Friends Committee on National Legislation, *Washington Newsletter*, July 1988.

The determining factor is not simply the unemployment rate. Unemployment and homelessness are certainly related: the more people without jobs, the more without homes. The history of successive periods of recession and fuller employment show a broad correlation. But, as in the case of the Depression, periods of high unemployment were expected to be followed by periods of low unemployment.

Today, there are fewer unemployed than there were in the mid-1970s, and the steady, significant rise in homelessness over the last 10 years is not paralleled by any similar steady rise in unemployment or the welfare rolls. No single indicator can adequately explain the startling rise in homelessness that we see today. Both the extent and the nature of employment and unemployment have changed, and so have the power relationships of employers and employees.

Deindustrialization is one part of these economic changes. The process is not a simple technological one involving a decline of manufacturing and rise of a service sector. There is nothing inherent in the service sector that dictates that its wages must be lower than those of the manufacturing sector. The fact that 44 percent of all new jobs created since 1980 pay poverty-level wages has as much to do with the relationship between employers and workers as with the type of work involved. The type of work may facilitate an aggrandizement of power by an employer, and may weaken the ability of a worker to insist on a decent wage, but it is ultimately conflict between the two that will decide how much is paid. The figures on the distribution of wealth show where things now stand: by 1983 the top 0.5 percent of US households owned 45 percent of all wealth (excluding personal residences), up 38 percent from twenty years earlier. And the gap between what they earn and what the poor earn is the greatest in history.

Marginalization of greater numbers of workers, and the accompanying loss of housing by the poorest among them is the ultimate result of conflicts among people, groups, classes, not of an undirected and uncontrolled march of technology, or of markets, or of organizational forms. And it is certainly not the result of some inexplicable change in "consumer preferences," as many of the popular accounts of the "revitalization of the city" would have us believe.

Masses of Unemployed

The surplus army of the unemployed is today more surplus than ever. Major segments of it are no longer relevant to the dominant processes of production. Larger and larger numbers of blacks, Hispanics, women, teenagers, the elderly, and the disabled are no longer necessary to the labor force. Maintaining their children is no longer necessary for the reproduction of the labor force, because they will never be "in" it. The homeless are the surplus of the surplus, the outer margin of the marginal.

Racism plays a substantial role in permitting such treatment of those forced to the economic margin. Were whites increasingly found sleeping on the streets, the questions raised would be sharper, the identification with the victims by the white middle class greater, the moral outrage more widespread, and the demands for action more immediate. But seeing black persons homeless fits in easily with white stereotyping, which makes blaming the victim easier. Thus, racism not only marginalizes minority group members disproportionately in the economic and housing systems, it also makes it more likely that, once homeless, they will stay that way. . . .

A thorough-going explanation of homelessness, finding its roots in the housing system, changes in employment patterns, and the spatial restructuring of cities, all abetted by governmental policies, has clear policy implications. First and foremost, *homelessness must be seen as a component, an extreme reflection, of general social, economic, and political patterns, not as an isolated problem, separate and apart.* . . .

The homeless themselves are continuing to organize, and their own demands reflect an awareness of the context in which they exist. In [homeless advocate] Chris Sprowal's words:

> If the government can send $100 million to some cutthroats in Central America then it can damn sure build some houses in this country. . . .

Such comments indicate why homelessness is such a danger to the legitimacy of the status quo. Homelessness in the midst of plenty may shock people into the realization that homelessness exists not because the system is failing to work as it should, but because the system *is* working as it must.

Recognizing Statements That Are Provable

From various sources of information we are constantly confronted with statements and generalizations about social and moral problems. In order to think clearly about these problems, it is useful if one can make a basic distinction between statements for which evidence can be found and other statements which cannot be verified or proved because evidence is not available, or the issue is so controversial that it cannot be definitely proved.

Readers should constantly be aware that magazines, newspapers, and other sources often contain statements of a controversial nature. The following activity is designed to allow experimentation with statements that are provable and those that are not. The following statements are taken from the viewpoints in this chapter. Consider each statement carefully. *Mark P for any statement you believe is provable. Mark U for any statement you feel is unprovable because of the lack of evidence. Mark C for any statements you think are too controversial to be proved to everyone's satisfaction.*

If you are doing this activity as a member of a class or group, compare your answers with those of other class or group members.

> P = *provable*
> U = *unprovable*
> C = *too controversial*

88

1. The top 0.5 percent of U.S. households owns 45 percent of the wealth.

2. The mentally ill are the most disturbing group of the homeless population.

3. Eight million American families now use half or more of their income to pay their rent or mortgage.

4. For poor people, family and friends have always meant survival.

5. The demand for emergency shelter increased by 20 percent nationwide in 1987.

6. It is probable that many of the homeless mentally ill would not be on the streets if they were on the caseload of a professional trained to deal with their problems.

7. More than half of the homeless men of the Bowery drink alcohol on a daily basis.

8. Homeless is a housing problem.

9. The label of mental illness places the destitute outside the sphere of ordinary life.

10. Only one-third of homeless people nationwide are mentally disabled.

11. Poverty plays a central role in the origins of family homelessness.

12. Nothing short of providing more low-income housing will solve the homelessness problem.

13. New York City mayor Ed Koch promised in 1988 that no one who sought refuge at a shelter would be turned away.

14. College professor Dan McMurry posed as a street person in 1988 as part of his research on homelessness.

15. Ignoring or concealing the problem of homelessness would be the easy way out.

16. Most of the men on skid row began drinking before they ended up there.

17. Racism not only marginalizes minority group members, it also makes it more likely that, once homeless, they will stay that way.

Periodical Bibliography

The following articles have been selected to supplement the diverse views presented in this chapter.

John R. Belcher and Jeff Singer	"Homelessness: A Cost of Capitalism," *Social Policy*, Spring 1988.
William R. Breakey	"Health and Mental Health Problems of Homeless Men and Women in Baltimore," *Journal of the American Medical Association*, September 4, 1989.
Warren T. Brookes	"Blaming Reagan for Homeless Exploitive," *Conservative Chronicle*, December 30, 1987. Available from *Conservative Chronicle*, Box 29, Hampton, IA 50441.
Warren T. Brookes	"There Is Not a Shortage of Available Housing," *Conservative Chronicle*, March 8, 1989.
C.C. Bruno	"Why I Am Homeless," *The Humanist*, May/June 1989.
The Futurist	"The New Poor: Jobless and Homeless in the U.S.," March/April 1986.
William Greider	"Gimme Shelter: Even Middle-Class Americans Now Feel the Housing Crisis," *Utne Reader*, May/June 1989.
Paul Koegel and M. Audrey Burnam	"Traditional and Nontraditional Homeless Alcoholics," *Alcohol Health and Research World*, Spring 1987. Available from the Superintendent of Documents, U.S. Government Printing Office, Washington, DC 20402.
Gina Kolata	"Drug Addicts Among the Homeless: Case Studies of Some 'Lost Dreams,'" *The New York Times*, May 30, 1989.
Gina Kolata	"Twins of the Streets: Homelessness and Addiction," *The New York Times*, May 22, 1989.
Gene McAnally	"I Was Homeless," *The Humanist*, May/June 1989.
Karin Ringheim	"Too Easy to Blame Addiction for Homelessness," *The New York Times*, June 12, 1989.

Should the Government Help the Homeless?

Chapter Preface

In the United States, a patchwork of private charities and organizations provide meals and shelter for the homeless. This could be called a tradition in the U.S., and no government agency has yet to fill this role. Yet many people, appalled by the growing number of homeless adults and families, are advocating a more active role for the federal government. This has led to controversies over whether such a role would be effective or is even necessary.

Authors Charles Hoch and Robert A. Slayton argue that increasing federal aid could actually increase homelessness. By paying the homeless for basics such as food and shelter, they believe, the homeless would have no incentive to struggle on their own with a minimum wage job.

Homeless activists and shelter organizers disagree with this view. To these people, the issue is a moral one. They believe that no one should be homeless in America and that society has an obligation to house and feed each one of its members.

These issues and others are debated in the following chapter.

"Why is government's response so inadequate? A commitment to other priorities, more rewarding to the business community that supports the present national political leadership."

The Government Should Do More for the Homeless

Peter Marcuse

Peter Marcuse is a professor of urban planning at Columbia University in New York City. In the following viewpoint, he argues that the government response to homelessness has been to understate the problem, to blame the victims, and to hide the homeless in emergency shelters. He contends that the government should ensure that there are jobs and houses for everyone.

As you read, consider the following questions:

1. Why does Marcuse believe the government's efforts to help the homeless have been ineffective?
2. Why does the government do so little to help the homeless, according to the author?
3. What does Marcuse contend is wrong with examining the homeless as part of a search for a solution?

Peter Marcuse, "Isolating the Homeless," *Shelterforce*, June/July 1988. Reprinted with permission.

Homelessness hit the headlines about 1981. When Kim Hopper and Ellen Baxter came out with their study of homelessness in New York, sponsored by the Community Service Society, it stirred up a wave of interest. They described in words and photos the experiences of those struggling to survive on the streets—sleeping on subway grates, eating handouts, using public bathrooms to wash, carrying all their possessions in a shopping cart or set of plastic bags.

More research uncovered worse. Some of the homeless suffered from serious mental health problems. Many should not be on the streets by themselves—more for their own safety than for the safety of others. Others were simply unemployed, taking occasional jobs when they could find them, but not scraping enough together to afford minimal shelter. Only 21% of a sample of shelter residents in 1985 had not worked at all in a three-year period. Twenty-nine percent were veterans. Seven percent of the occupants of emergency shelters (not family shelters) were unemployed and under the age of 21—that was unheard of 10 years earlier. Eighty-nine percent were Black or Hispanic. The most rapidly increasing group were mothers and children. The majority of the homeless in shelters were there almost every night over a five-month period—homelessness was no longer a short-term or "emergency" problem.

Reports from other cities confirmed the pattern as a national one. The National Coalition for the Homeless estimated 20,000 homeless in Baltimore, 15,000 in Philadelphia, 25,000 in Houston, 14,000 in Dallas, 5,000 in Phoenix, 10,000 in San Francisco, and 50,000 in Los Angeles for July, 1986. . . .

Inadequate Response

Government's response has borne almost no relationship to the problem at any level—federal, state, or city. Homelessness is not a federal responsibility according to Ronald Reagan. In the District of Columbia, where the Federal government has no one else to whom to pass the buck, it has provided the barest of shelters since 1984. It took a 51 day hunger strike and militant protests by the homeless and their advocates and a flair for public relations to force any kind of constructive movement at all. The largest single success that the movement for the homeless has had to date, the passage of the McKinney Act, provides limited funds for a variety of separate programs and ignores the need for major additions to the housing stock to provide permanent opportunities for the homeless.

At the state and local levels the picture is no brighter. The best programs remain "pilot" programs, small in scale, dubbed "experimental," tenuously funded, effected only through the extraordinary efforts of committed volunteers and activists. The majority of programs provide at best a shelter for the night, generally ousting users at or before breakfast and not permitting their return till nightfall; assuming that somehow, somewhere, their residents will find other accommodations in the near future and not be seen again. In fact, the hope that somehow the homeless will go away is an undercurrent that runs through almost all official programs "for the homeless." Whether sheltered or not, if the homeless were simply not visible, not obtrusive, not on the streets where upstanding citizens are confronted by their presence, most local leaders would consider the problem solved.

Building on Fear

The NIMBY syndrome (Not In My Back Yard) of course plays into their hands. Where social service-type facilities are concerned (half-way houses, drug rehabilitation clinics, etc.) it often turns out that the objections are not so much to the facility but the manner of its planning and operation. Neighbors are not consulted in planning, management is inadequate, security is not provided, local facilities are overloaded, some areas are saturated with difficult facilities while others are exempted. When neighbors object, they are accused of not wanting the facility in their community. Local leaders are quick to take advantage of NIMBY objections and use them as an excuse for inaction, instead of dealing with the legitimate problems they reflect.

Possible Remedies

Government actions aggravating homelessness must be turned around. Homelessness caused by gentrification and abandonment involve changes that can readily be avoided by available land-use control devices, perhaps with some imaginative modifications. Provisions against displacement, antiwarehousing measures, controls on condominium and cooperative conversions, public reinvestment in abandoned neighborhoods, the use of tax-abatement and exemption policies to promote integration rather than gentrification, an equitable distribution of public services and facilities, and antidisplacement zoning are all among the possibilities.

Peter Marcuse, *Christianity and Crisis*, April 18, 1988.

Why is government's response so inadequate? A commitment to other priorities, more rewarding to the business community that supports the present national political leadership. Running government like a business suggests that an investment in housing the homeless is not productive. Contracts to build missiles or permits to build office towers are much more rewarding for those currently in power than subsidies for the homeless.

Pure stupidity contributes to the inadequacy of government's response. President Reagan at one of his infrequent press conferences remarked, "I just read this morning in the paper about a needy family in New York that is being put up in a hotel, and the cost to welfare just for the rent of the hotel room is $37,000 a year. And I wonder why somebody doesn't build them a house for $37,000."

In fact it is the federal policy that led to money being spent for welfare hotels (which is half federal emergency assistance money) instead of going into permanent housing (even apart from the fact that the median cost of a house in 1986 was over $75,000, and of a newly-built house over $100,000).

But neither penury, petty graft, political opportunism, nor stupidity are sufficient to account for what is happening. Let me suggest a more fundamental explanation.

Uncomfortable Questions

Homelessness is shocking. It shocks most people to see someone homeless, not so much because they visualize themselves as in danger of being homeless, but because of what homelessness says about the society in which we live. Isn't homelessness something we associate with Third World countries, not with our own? What is going on here anyway, that something like this can exist? Such questions can be dangerous.

The shock of homelessness leads to other uncomfortable questions. The private market, the conservative myth goes, is the best supplier of housing. Will the private market conceivably supply housing for the homeless? Are not the homeless without homes precisely because they cannot contribute to any landlord's profits, to any builder's sales, to any realtor's commissions? Does not the private market in fact cause much of the recent growth of homelessness through skyrocketing rents, the gentrification of neighborhoods, the conversion to other uses of the former homes of the presently homeless? Homelessness exists not because something is wrong in the housing system, but because the system is working as it is expected to.

What really are the economic alternatives open to the homeless? Would more training help? Then why did the Reagan administration end the National Support Work Program in 1981, designed precisely to help the "hardcore poor" enter the labor market effectively? Are there decent jobs available for them, even with additional training? Permanent unemployment is now an accepted feature of our economy, and 44% of the new jobs created lie at poverty-level wages, compared to less than 20% of the preceding two decades. Such questions lead to thoughts of full employment policies, preventing plant closings, minimum wages and job guarantees—dangerous thoughts with which a conservative establishment would rather not have to deal. If our society really

© Shelly/Rothco Cartoons

cannot afford to put a roof over the heads of 3,000,000 people in our own country, can it spend hundreds of billions of dollars on a questionable Star Wars defense? What kind of priorities does our national budget really reflect? . . .

Blaming the Victim

If denial won't work in the face of everyday observations, then blame the victim. As the homespun wisdom has it, the homeless are not like you and me. There's something wrong with them or they wouldn't be homeless. They're incompetent, crazies, drunks, drug addicts, kooks. They're dirty, unpleasant, queer, different. They're social problems—we have other more worthy social problems to worry about.

The academic version is more dangerous. To get at the roots of homelessness, inquire who the homeless are. Some have mental problems. They need medical care. Others have a substance abuse problem. Put them into a detoxification program. Many are children. Teach their mothers morality or, for non-Catholics, birth control. Some are evicted because they can't pay the rent. Well, what can you do? Give them housing temporarily, but they just have to learn that the landlord comes first. Homelessness is merely the sum of the special problems of particular deviants. Gone from consideration are the issues of the housing shortage, unemployment, cutbacks in social programs, gentrification and condominium conversions, escalating rents and housing-for-profit only.

Hide the consequences is the third line of defense. If some action has to be taken because of protest or court order, let it serve to move the problem out of sight, out of people's daily awareness so they can ignore its implications with a good conscience. Let the homeless be warehoused in emergency shelters in remote areas of town, out of sight, out of mind.

Unfortunately, much of the media and philanthropic concern have lent themselves to these approaches. The shocking nature of the situation does not permit it to be ignored. The question is, how is it handled when it is covered? The upsurge in attention is beyond doubt. There have been specials on public television, constant coverage in *The New York Times*. It's even become acceptable material for prime-time TV.

Toward Solutions

But the bulk of the coverage treats homelessness as a special human interest story and focuses on who the homeless are. The human interest, of course, is there. The homeless are human—to lose sight of their humanity in the debate over abstract policies might win the battle and lose the war. But you can't understand the cause of homelessness by examining the homeless, unless you believe they bring it on themselves.

What ought to be done is quite clear.

• First, housing for the homeless is of three types: immediate emergency but short-term shelter; transitional housing with support and social services as needed; and permanent housing. Without permanent housing in sufficient quantity, of decent quality, in coordinated fashion, "emergency" and "transitional" housing is hypocrisy. There is a growing movement against anything less than permanent housing as a governmental response to homelessness.

• Second, homes (for the homeless and for everyone else) have to be seen as more than just shelter, and neighborhood conditions have to be made livable in all areas, services provided, facilities created, to meet the needs of residents. Where those needs are more severe, the services need to be broader, with government responding to need as it was created to do.

• Third, homelessness has to be seen as part of a general housing problem. A general housing policy has to be developed that will deal with expanding supply, holding down costs (and that means profits), and making it available on a fair and non-discriminatory basis.

• Fourth, ultimately, public control has to be exercised over economic development in the country, so that the jobs created and the benefits received are shared more widely and more equitably. Treating homelessness as a subject for charitable benevolence hardly helps to move in these directions.

2 VIEWPOINT

"A federal takeover of the homelessness problem, with gushing federal dollars . . .will do little to help."

The Government Should Not Do More for the Homeless

Kenneth J. Beirne

The problem of homelessness in America is exaggerated, according to Kenneth J. Beirne. Homelessness can be adequately addressed by local governments and by charities, he argues, without the need for federal action. Charities can respond by opening more shelters, he contends, while local governments can prevent the destruction of low-income housing. Beirne is a former general deputy assistant secretary for policy development and research at the Department of Housing and Urban Development. He is an adjunct scholar at The Heritage Foundation, a conservative think tank in Washington, D.C.

As you read, consider the following questions:

1. Why does Beirne argue that homelessness should be addressed on a local level?
2. What does the author believe is dangerous about exaggerating the problem of homelessness?

Kenneth J. Beirne, "America's Homeless: A Manageable Problem and Solution," The Heritage Foundation *Backgrounder Update*, May 4, 1987. Reprinted with permission.

America's homeless problem is manageable. Studies of a number of cities reinforce the 1984 estimate of the U.S. Department of Housing and Urban Development that, on any given night, approximately 300,000 Americans are homeless. Currently there are shelters and emergency beds available to house about half this number. Already, however, private agencies, states, and localities have been providing extra resources at a rapid rate to meet specific, local needs. It is likely that the remaining problem of homelessness can be met with a modest expansion of existing efforts, combined with specialized assistance to the mentally ill, who account for up to half the homeless population.

Needless Panic

Congress is being needlessly panicked into acting without thinking. Lawmakers are ignoring the mounting evidence concerning the actual size and nature of the homeless problem. Cynical posturing by local politicians and sensational news reports have combined to create legislative momentum for largely irrelevant federal programs, based on the myth that there is a growing population of over two million homeless Americans who are overwhelming local agencies. Only massive infusions of federal cash, say advocates, can deal with the problem. The truth is that there is no basis for the two million figure. To make matters worse, such reckless projections discourage those local actions that are actually making significant progress.

Homelessness is a problem whose best solution draws on the strength of decentralized federalism. It is not an issue that demands centralized funding and control. Studies indicate that the characteristics of the homeless population differ significantly from city to city. In no American city does the number of homeless appear to exceed the resources of state, local, and private agencies—especially once the unique problems of the mentally ill are addressed. What is required is not more top-down money, but clear local resolve and the energetic use of existing resources in the affected areas.

The Administration and Congress can serve the homeless most effectively in three ways:

1) Modifying existing law and regulations to make sure that the mentally ill are not deinstitutionalized and put out on to the street without adequate local care already in place.

2) Continuing to eliminate restrictions on housing and community programs that prevent cities from serving the homeless under existing programs and make it difficult for state and local agencies to coordinate services.

3) Preventing the use of federal funds to tear down single occupancy hotels and other housing for low-income Americans. . . .

In the years since the publication of a 1984 HUD report

estimating the homeless population at 250,000 to 350,000, the study remains the only scientific and comprehensive attempt at a national estimate of homelessness. A number of localized but more intensive studies not only have confirmed HUD's description of the homeless population, but also have supported the accuracy of HUD's estimate of the size of the homeless population. In fact, studies of New York, Chicago, and Los Angeles, the three cities generally acknowledged to have the largest homeless populations, lead to the conclusion that, if anything, HUD may have overstated the number of homeless significantly. Examples:

A September 1986 study undertaken for the National Bureau of Economic Research (NBER), a highly respected data analysis group, concludes that HUD's national numbers for New York City were reasonably accurate. The study did somewhat disagree regarding the characteristics of the homeless, finding much more long-term homelessness in the city, but otherwise the analysis did not fault the HUD study. NBER interviews with the homeless indicate not only the usual information about the prevalence of mental illness and substance abuse, but also the presence of criminal backgrounds as a strong causal element—a factor rarely noted. The description of the New York homeless makes clear that the characteristics and relative size of the homeless population differ markedly from city to city.

Local Management

Federal programs are extraordinarily splintered. That would be bad news were it not for the fact that most of the management of homelessness is occurring at the local level. One of the Reagan Administration's policies has been to assume that the local level is substantially able to handle the homeless problem, unless the problem should prove to be of a prohibitive size. And nothing in the evidence so far indicates that it is of a size that would prohibit localities from handling it.

Kenneth J. Beirne, *Rethinking Policy on Homelessness*, 1989.

A 1986 study by the University of Chicago and the University of Massachusetts-Amherst indicates a nightly Chicago homeless population of fewer than 3,000 persons. The HUD estimate three years earlier had been approximately 20,000. The Chicago study was based on intensive street survey work and shelter interviews, and concludes that "[the smaller numbers] are the only estimates based on actual counts of homeless persons, conducted according to scientific sampling practices."

Los Angeles. Los Angeles has been subject to a number of studies since 1983. A 1984 study by the Los Angeles Department of Mental Health in the most concentrated area of homelessness, Skid Row, confirmed only 7,000 homeless; the HUD study had put the citywide number at 31,000 to 33,000, which would have required 15,000 to 20,000 homeless in Skid Row. The 1986 Los Angeles analysis of the Skid Row area, using an intense, scientific methodology similar to that of the Chicago study, arrived at a single night estimate of fewer than 2,500.

False Assumption

Both HUD's study and the New York study assumed that the number of homeless outside shelters was approximately double the number inside. But actual counts in Chicago, Los Angeles, Denver, Washington, and Nashville all find less than one person outside a shelter for each inside. This change in the comparative figures is in large part a result of strenuous efforts by city officials and shelter managers to find homeless Americans and bring them in off the streets. In many cases, the homeless are very reluctant to stay in shelters. Where the city studies can be compared to the HUD estimates, this and other factors resulted in figures less than one-third of the HUD estimates.

No serious city study of homelessness, except for the New York study, has come up with a figure anywhere near as high as HUD's. And HUD's numbers are much lower than the shocking "estimates" routinely cited in the press, on television, and at congressional hearings. . . .

Only if the problem is presented in honest and realistic terms such that it appears manageable, warns Martha Hicks, who heads the Skid Row Development Corporation in Los Angeles, "[will] people want to help because they feel they can really make a difference."

Local Efforts

Local governments and private agencies have increased significantly their efforts to deal with homelessness. The 1984 HUD report found a 41 percent increase in the number of shelters in just the four years prior to the report. The study also found that 94 percent of shelters were operated by charitable and other private organizations. Between 1980 and 1986, for instance, the number of shelters in Massachusetts jumped from merely two to 29. Denver maintains 1,000 shelter beds and supplemental rooms in boardinghouses and hotels to handle a homeless population, which a recent study counted as 1,200 to 1,500 persons. And since 1980, Los Angeles has opened new shelters providing 1,200 beds to supplement 1,000 beds in mission shelters in the Skid Row area alone.

Governments at all levels have stepped up efforts to tackle the problem. Example: HUD records indicate that cities have used over $112 million of federal Community Development Block

Grant (CDBG) funds for homelessness since 1983. This probably understates the actual amount spent, since the reporting is voluntary and not part of usual record requirements. Among a number of state initiatives, Illinois responded to the Chicago study by raising its appropriations for the homeless.

Toward a Coherent Policy

To a very great extent, as they got a serious idea of what has to be done to deal with homelessness, the localities have started to move more and more to the provision of services to the homeless. They are focusing on bringing the homeless into mental health programs, family assistance programs, or other programs for which they may be eligible. By making that transition, the localities are moving rapidly in what looks to be a coherent policy direction, and in the typical fashion, leaving the federal government behind.

Kenneth J. Beirne, *Rethinking Policy on Homelessness*, 1989.

At the federal level, meanwhile, as early as 1983, HUD, the Department of Defense, and the General Services Administration acted to provide underutilized federally owned buildings to cities and charitable organizations for temporary use as homeless shelters. These federal agencies continue to work with communities to keep facilities available. HUD set up simplified procedures for public housing agencies, making it easier for them to make emergency housing available for homeless families. And since 1983, the Federal Emergency Food and Shelter program has disbursed $210 million for homeless assistance through the states and a national board of charitable organizations. The limited and general nature of the federal measures properly has kept the focus on local initiative and the unique nature of each homeless problem. . . .

The Best Response

Homelessness is a problem for which the American multilayered federal system is well suited. Homelessness is not rampant and overwhelming. With the possible exception of New York City, it is manageable using the resources of state, local, and private agencies, together with existing federally funded programs for which there is local discretion. The New York problem is clearly linked to the city's destruction of its own housing supply through rent and development controls and exacerbated by City Hall's policy of holding on to tens of thousands of unrehabilitated vacant apartments.

Depending on the makeup of the homeless population, the best response in other cities includes land use policies that encourage single room occupancy hotels, rather than tearing them down, and provides emergency housing vouchers for families. . . .

If federal, state, and local governments are to work with the private sector in serving the homeless whose needs can be addressed by normal means, they need to continue their current efforts based on local initiatives. Private agencies, charitable organizations, and churches should continue to play the primary role in providing services, supplemented by governments. This is a problem of a size and character precisely suited to be handled within the federal system, using existing resources.

A federal takeover of the homelessness problem, with gushing federal dollars and regulations, replacing creative local efforts, may enable some members of Congress to appear compassionate, and it will assure a direct money pipeline for the media star homeless advocates. But it will do little to help the creative local groups on the frontline of the issue—or the homeless themselves.

"Government creates homelessness and shelter dependency when it provides too little money even to pay the rent."

Increasing Welfare Benefits Would Reduce Homelessness

Peter Rossi

Peter Rossi is a professor of sociology at the University of Massachusetts in Amherst. In the following viewpoint, he argues that inflation has lowered the real value of welfare benefits since the 1960s, leaving many welfare recipients unable to pay their rent. He contends that increasing the poor's welfare payments would enable them to rent apartments and avoid homelessness.

As you read, consider the following questions:

1. What would offset the costs of increasing welfare benefits, according to Rossi?
2. What program does the author suggest to provide benefits for homeless adults?
3. How would Rossi ensure that only poor households would benefit from these measures?

The important questions to be asked, before deciding on programs to address the problem of homelessness, are: Why are some kinds of people more likely than others to be homeless? And why has homelessness increased so sharply over the past decade? . . .

So long as there is a poverty population whose incomes put them on the economic edge, there will be people who fall, periodically, over that edge and into a state of homelessness. The solution is to develop provisions in the social welfare system that would protect against short-term economic difficulties.

What of the chronically homeless, the one in four who has been homeless for two or more years and who appears likely to continue in that condition for a much longer period? The distinguishing characteristics of the long-term homeless are their extraordinarily high levels of disabilities of all sorts, incapacities that impair their earning power, diminish their employment prospects, and reduce their acceptance by families, kin, and friends. These are the persons most strongly and directly affected by shortages of unskilled positions in the labor force, by the loss of inexpensive housing, and by declines in the economic fortunes of their social networks. . . .

No Quick Fixes

What, then, is to be done? The very impressive increase in researchers' knowledge of homelessness does not suggest any quick fixes or instant remedies. Homelessness in the larger sense may well be here for decades and may never be totally erased, largely because the problem results, as noted, from large-scale societal developments that are not likely to be rolled back. Still, being able to assure that no one involuntarily goes without nightly shelter, even if that shelter may not fulfill all our ideal definitions of *home*, is a realistic aspiration. And it is also a reasonable goal to reduce to the absolute minimum the number of individuals and families whose living situations fall short of the security, stability, safety, and privacy that are associated with the larger meaning of *home*. . . .

A set of recommendations concerns the holes in the social welfare safety net. At present, benefit programs provide mainly for the aged, for the families of dependent children, and for those who have recognized, "traditional" disabilities—such as blindness or partial paralysis. Aging people, dependent children, and the physically disabled arouse considerable sympathy on the part of legislatures and the larger public, who respond magnanimously to the needs of these groups. The nation has yet to fully recognize other forms of disability that are equally damaging to an individual's capacity to participate fully in our society, especially in the labor force. . . .

Our society consistently underestimates the importance of income, especially to the poor, often mistaking the effects of poverty for the effects of personal deficiencies. Nothing seemed more dismal to those researching the old Skid Rows in the 1960s than the apparent and utter hopelessness of the aged pensioners found there. Few, if any, advocated raising old-age pensions to ameliorate their inadequate living conditions. Yet, as the value of old-age pensions rose in the subsequent decades, the drop in the number and proportion of aged persons among the homeless was dramatic. Provided with a reasonable level of income, the generations who became elderly in the 1970s and 1980s were spared the fate of becoming homeless.

Persistent Poverty

A restructuring economy combined with cutbacks in public welfare benefits in the early 1980s shifted the worst economic hardships accompanying the recession of those years onto the working poor. Social Security, Medicare, and unemployment insurance, despite their many limitations, did insulate otherwise vulnerable segments of the working and middle classes from the trauma of destitution. The growing numbers of poor people were not so fortunate. They received fewer welfare benefits as well because of cutbacks in AFDC, food stamps, and child nutritional programs. The problems of unemployment, underemployment, and inadequate welfare benefits have tended to accumulate in the 1980s for those at the bottom of the class hierarchy, weakening their economic security and increasing their susceptibility to homelessness. Ultimately, fundamental changes in the domestic economy as well as welfare programs are needed to remedy the inequalities that make poverty a persistent and deplorable condition in a society with the resources capable of putting an end to it.

David C. Schwartz, Richard C. Ferlauto, and Daniel N. Hoffman, *A New Housing Policy for America*, 1988.

The lesson of what higher benefits accomplished for the aged may be applied to many other categories of today's homeless population. I have documented the severe deterioration in AFDC [Aid to Families with Dependent Children] and GA [General Assistance] benefits over the past two decades. Inflation has lowered the real value of these payments to the point where recipients are not raised to a level that is even near the poverty level. This deterioration in support for families and individuals undoubtedly increased homelessness and changed the composition of the homeless population. Government creates homelessness and shelter dependency when it provides too little money even to pay the rent. Society creates more homelessness by placing the burden on poor families to provide support for their unemployed—sometimes unemployable—adult members. We foster long-term shelter dependency when we fail to provide long-term unemployed, single, unattached persons with enough money to rent better accommodations. All of these changes have shifted the age structure of the homeless downward and have increased the proportion of minorities among the homeless.

Increasing Benefits

There are two remedies for these problems. The first is as simple to implement as it is expensive: restore the value of welfare benefits that have been so seriously eroded by inflation over the past twenty years. This would restore the ability of many among the poor to cope more effectively with the housing market. It is a shameful irony that New York's welfare department pays three to four times the going rent for low-cost apartments to welfare hotels to house single-parent families who are homeless because they cannot rent apartments on their inadequate welfare benefits.

There is some substantive evidence that the American public would favor such a move. In a 1986 national survey conducted by the National Opinion Research Center, a sample-survey research unit affiliated with the University of Chicago, respondents favored awarding to single-parent families benefits that were several times those currently in place. Although the average payment under AFDC was $325 per month in 1985, survey respondents awarded $1,152 per month to AFDC-eligible families, more than 3.5 times the current benefit level. The American public apparently understands inflation and its consequences better than do its legislators.

Current AFDC expenditures run about $15 billion annually. Restoring the ravages of inflation over the past two decades would involve a 60 percent increase to $24 billion. Offsetting some of these costs are the savings to be realized by the resulting improved health status of both mothers and children, the bolstering of the lower end of the rental housing market by firming up demand, and the increased expenditures for other consumer goods.

Support for Families

The second remedy is more difficult because it entails subsidies for categories of families and persons that have not historically received welfare support. The recommendation is to provide direct support to families who subsidize their destitute, unattached adult members—in effect, *Aid to Families with Dependent Adults*. The purpose of such a program is obvious: to help poor families provide housing, food, and other amenities to their adult members who cannot support themselves. This might take a variety of forms. For example, if the GA payment to a destitute adult is, say, three hundred dollars per month, an additional payment could be provided directly to any primary kin providing a home to that adult.

Another alternative is to split benefit payments, part going to the recipient and part going to caretakers. . . . To assure that government spending for this would be concentrated on poor households, the benefit payments to households should be taxed as income.

Matt Wuerker, reprinted by permission.

It would be difficult to exaggerate the difficulties of defining such a program and administering it. Benefit programs traditionally have been addressed to persons either before maturity or beyond ordinary working years. Indeed, the very title of AFDC emphasizes that the benefits are being made for the sake of the children involved, underemphasizing the fact that support for adults in their working years is also being supplied. The program here has as its target adults in their working years who do not have responsibility for children, a group that society has not been generous to in the past. However, legislators and the public might react with sympathy for the families who have taken on the burdens of supporting dependent adults and would look with more sympathy on a program that would help to ease those burdens.

The extent of adult dependency is surprisingly large. In 1987, the Current Population Survey estimated that there were some 4.9 million unmarried, childless persons between the ages of twenty-two and fifty-nine who were neither students nor living on farms and whose 1986 incomes were under four thousand dollars. Three million earned less than two thousand dollars. The majority (60 percent) lived with parents or siblings, the remainder either alone (20 percent) or with nonrelatives (20 percent). Many of these unattached adults were only temporarily destitute: in March 1987, when the survey was conducted, a third were employed.

If the eligibility requirements of the program are set so that an unattached adult must have an income under four thousand dollars for at least eighteen months before becoming eligible, and that as many as 1 million would probably be eligible for benefits under disability programs, then approximately 2-2.5 million would likely qualify. Assuming benefits that amounted to six thousand dollars per year or five hundred dollars per month, the benefit payments would amount to $12 to $15 billion annually. The net cost would be offset to some degree by the increased tax liabilities of the host households.

Difficult but Necessary

A critical point of the proposal is that the benefits be shared between the unattached person and that person's family if they share a household. The immediate problem encountered is the need to define which kinship relationships are "family": certainly parents and children would qualify, as would siblings. More distant kin, such as grandparents and parents' siblings, are problematic. I suggest that family be narrowly confined to parents, children, and siblings, including step- or foster versions. Another difficulty surrounds how to split and deliver the payments, and that must be left to the experts in the design of payment systems.

Finally, there is the problem of how to strip such a benefit system of unintended disincentives. For example, the system should encourage dependent adults to become employed, possibly by tapering off payments to beneficiaries rather than abruptly terminating them when they become employed. The program also ought to encourage the formation of new households, but only if there is some assurance that the new household will not simply become a beneficiary of some other program. Of course, programs of this kind are difficult to administer and subject to abuse, but if we abandoned all programs of which that might be said, we would never accomplish anything.

"For the ... chronically homeless, the answer to their situation lies not in bringing them back into a larger welfare system ... but in bringing them back into society."

Increasing Welfare Benefits Would Not Reduce Homelessness

C. Brandon Crocker

In the following viewpoint, C. Brandon Crocker argues that increasing welfare benefits to the homeless would make the homeless too dependent on welfare and reduce their incentive to be productive members of society. Crocker contends that only by encouraging the homeless to work and to be independent will the problem of homelessness be solved. Crocker is a financial planner in San Diego, California and a contributor to the *California Review*, a monthly conservative newspaper published by students in the University of California system.

As you read, consider the following questions:

1. How does the author answer the charge that economic factors cause homelessness?
2. Why are the homeless harmed by the welfare system, according to Crocker?
3. What alternatives does Crocker offer to increasing welfare benefits?

C. Brandon Crocker, "Thoughts on the Homeless," *California Review*, October 1988. Reprinted with the author's permission.

An acquaintance of mine, who is an animal rights advocate, recently put forth the proposition to me that the problem of the homeless can be solved by substituting the homeless for animals in laboratory experiments. An interesting suggestion, but one that I had to reject. Perhaps I read too much Locke in my formative years.

Any serious proposal to alleviate the homeless problem must be based on the facts of the situation. First we have to answer the question, what is the magnitude of the problem? How many homeless are there? Then we have to explore the question of who are the homeless. Only then can we start to determine what effectiveness certain proposals might have.

The Numbers Question

The question of the number of homeless in this country is very difficult to answer. Most of the numbers batted around have absolutely no factual support. The only meaning these numbers have, therefore, is to tell you the political persuasion of the people using them. For instance, in 1984 the Department of Housing and Urban Development released a flimsy study estimating the homeless population at 250,000 to 350,000. On the other hand, left-wing activists use a figure of 2 to 3 million (or about 1% of the population). . . .

As far as being able to pin an exact number on the homeless, we will have to admit defeat, except to say that the number is not insignificant.

Now, from where do these not insignificant numbers come? According to Robert Hayes, Executive Director of the National Coalition for the Homeless, the homeless phenomenon is the result of "a cruel economy, an unresponsive government, [and] a festering value system." A lot of people who . . . hate Capitalism in general agree. These people are holding up the homeless as victims of elements beyond their control, but within the control of the government.

A Fair and Just Economy

A coalition of Leftist groups and liberal Democrats are using the homeless issue and the homeless themselves, in a lobbying effort to achieve one of their shared goals—changing our "national economic priorities" (i.e. slashing defense spending and raising taxes on the "rich" and corporations to fund a massive expansion of social programs).

The facts, however, do not support the view that a "cruel" economy is the "cause" of homelessness (or in Jesse Jackson's words "economic violence" perpetrated by the Reagan administration). The economy has been expanding, with 17 million jobs created since 1983 (paying on average $22,000). Unemployment is at its lowest since 1974. Furthermore, a University of Michigan study has demolished the charge that the poor keep getting poorer and the rich even richer due to a rigid and unfair economic system. On the contrary, the study shows the U.S. economy to be healthily endowed with that virtue of Capitalism—economic mobility.

The Real Causes

So what *has* caused the homeless problem? The homeless, like most any group, is varied, but beyond any doubt a large portion (approximately 35% by most respected observations) are the mentally ill, which have been turned out of mental institutions over the past two decades, mainly because the states did not want to pay for them anymore.

Of the homeless who are not mentally ill, many tell stories centering around the death or running away of their spouse, followed by depression and heavy use of alcohol, causing them to lose their job, and then falling into their current condition. These are unfortunate stories, indeed, but they don't tell of a "cruel economy." Many others have been jobless most or all of their adult lives and do not actively seek full-time employment. Some of the homeless have been recently laid off and are in search of new jobs and low income housing. But those in this last category, for the most part, appear to be homeless for only short periods of time and do not keep reappearing at shelters.

The Homeless Underclass

The sizable underclass contingent among the homeless—not just among the welfare mothers but also among the drunks and drug abusers—serves as a cautionary reminder of the unintended consequences of social programs. The underclass is the starkest example of the hydralike quality of some social problems, growing worse and more intractable as a result of the efforts made to solve them. The underclass's entrenched culture of dependence, its inability from one generation to another to participate in the larger society, the stunted development of its human potentialities—all this was fostered by the welfare system and the War on Poverty.

Myron Magnet, *Fortune*, November 23, 1987.

Furthermore, the conglomeration which makes up most of the chronically homeless—the mentally ill and those who have withdrawn from society through the use of drugs and alcohol—is not a group of people who fell through "holes" in the safety net— they jumped off the safety net. Either through an inability to understand the welfare system, or through a deliberate turning away from society, these people have not taken advantage of programs *already in place* that would relieve their homeless situation. (In 1979 the *average* welfare family of four received $18,000 worth of subsidies. And welfare spending per capita has continued to grow even through the Reagan years.) An expanded system will not help the homeless; it will only help current and would-be members of the welfare bureaucracy.

If more welfare is not the answer, what is? Obviously addressing the problem of the mentally ill would go a long way in shrinking the homeless problem. Certainly, many people with mental disabilities are able to care for themselves outside of institutions. But it is also obvious, however, that those mentally ill people who are unable to hold down a job, make use of government services, and are otherwise unable to look after normal day to day functions which would keep them off the street, do need to be institutionalized—both for their own protection and for the protection of public health. . . .

Teaching Independence

As for the rest of the chronically homeless, the answer to their situation lies not in bringing them back into a larger welfare system than that which they have already foregone, where they develop a psychological dependence, but in bringing them back into society, and developing in them a feeling of self-worth. The first step in achieving this is recognizing as a society that the responsibility of caring for oneself lies with the individual. By convincing the homeless that they are victims of the economic system, they will in fact become victims of a welfare system which enslaves them to a life of public dependence and poverty. If those working with the homeless don't expect the population with which they deal to better their circumstances through their own diligence, the homeless will develop the same attitude.

In fact, there is growing evidence that this is happening. Says Mike Elias, a former member of the homeless who runs a shelter in Los Angeles, "I've got to brainwash [people who come from other shelters] to let them know that, hey, you can stand on your own two feet; you don't have to be standing around going from church to church, agency to agency, getting handouts."

This is the proper way to combat homelessness—treat the homeless as responsible human beings who *can* change their situations, not as helpless victims who cannot be expected to help themselves. Mike Elias' philosophy, however, as he expressed it to a reporter at *Insight* magazine is not popular with his colleagues. "I'm saying 'Homeless people, you've got the power within yourselves to get on your feet and get going.' And my colleagues in the business are saying, 'No, it's because—' and they list them. They attack the states, the counties, the cities, the federal government, whatever.'' He continues ''When I talk about the dignity of the human being and getting up and working, I am booed out.'' As long as this remains a prevalent attitude among social workers, we will never solve the problem of chronic homelessness.

Wittingly or not, the road taken by Elias' antagonists, taking the primary responsibility for one's homelessness off of the individual, is helping to form a permanent class of homeless people, forever reliant on others and driven into hopelessness that robs them of their will to break the bonds of dependence. But, of course, they will always sound more compassionate than the Mike Eliases of the world.

"Intervention, sheltered housing and treatment are needed to attack the underlying causes of the desperate and demeaning condition [of homelessness]."

The Government Should Support Shelters

Edwin M. Conway

Father Edwin M. Conway is administrator of Catholic Charities of the Archdiocese of Chicago. Catholic Charities provides a variety of social programs, including shelters for the homeless. The following viewpoint is taken from Conway's testimony before the House Subcommittee on Banking, Finance, and Urban Affairs. In it, Conway argues for more shelters and services to meet the needs of the homeless. He contends that developing shelters which provide job training as well as a place to live could enable the homeless to lead independent lives.

As you read, consider the following questions:

1. What does Conway believe is misleading about studies which count the number of people who spend the night in shelters in order to estimate the size of the homeless population?
2. What two groups make up the homeless, in the author's opinion?
3. What additional programs does Conway recommend to help the homeless?

Edwin N. Conway, "The Forms of Homelessness," *Origins*, February 26, 1987.

I am Father Edwin M. Conway, administrator of the Catholic Charities of the Archdiocese of Chicago and treasurer of Catholic Charities USA. We appreciate the invitation to testify today on a problem which imposes a heavy burden of suffering on many of our citizens: the problem of homelessness.

Catholic Charities of Chicago is a comprehensive human service agency serving Cook and Lake counties in Illinois. This year we will provide services to approximately 570,000 individuals in all sorts of need. Catholic Charities of Chicago is the largest of the 600 human service agencies and 200 specialized institutions which are federated under the flag of Catholic Charities USA. Most of these institutions provide emergency assistance in the form of shelter, clothing and food, as well as advocacy and legal assistance to people in crisis. Today I want to illuminate the situations of these agencies and the people they serve through a presentation of our experience in Chicago rendering assistance to the homeless. . . .

A Necessary Program

We share the concern of those who feel that the government should not institutionalize an emergency program. But our experience around the country tells us that the problem has not yet gone away; indeed, the misery of families coming into our agencies makes us urge the continuation of this program.

Homelessness in Chicago is a serious and worsening problem, though its scope and magnitude are poorly understood. Estimates of the number of people who find themselves without housing at some time over the course of a year range from 5,000 to 25,000. Only one scientific study has been made, and this produced a low estimate: 4,000 to 6,000 homeless over the course of a year, 1,600 to 3,100 on any one night. This study, however, employed an excessively restrictive definition of homelessness and a correspondingly narrow sampling methodology so that it measured only the number of people who spend the night either in shelters or in public places.

In truth, homeless people spend their nights in many other places. They spend them primarily in the homes of friends, relatives and acquaintances; in motels and flophouses; in church basements and spare rectory bedrooms; and in their cars. They also spend them hidden in culverts and under viaducts, in dangerous abandoned buildings and on rooftops; in railroad cars and truck trailers; and in a thousand other places where social scientists would not dare to visit but where homeless folk are desperate and ingenious enough to take refuge.

The extent of homelessness in Chicago, then, has not yet been credibly measured. But beyond a doubt, it is very much greater than 6,000 people over the course of a year, and in any case it vastly overwhelms existing efforts to address its underlying causes or even to shelter its victims. This is the experience of Catholic Charities and other Catholic service providers in Chicago.

Catholic Charities offers shelter to many different homeless populations, targeted by a variety of different types of shelters and residential programs.

The Hard-Core Homeless

First of all, we operate two emergency overnight shelters with a total capacity of 169 beds on the old Skid Row west of the Loop. These shelters are always full. Two other overnight shelters of 188 and 40 beds are maintained by Franciscan Fathers and Dominican Fathers in other depressed areas of the city. These shelters have slightly lower average occupancy rates, but on cold nights they are full and must turn away 10 to 590 applicants each. These turnaway counts are understated, however, because word spreads rapidly on the street that the shelters are full, and many who would avail themselves if there were room are discouraged before reaching the doors.

National Estimates of the Number of Homeless Shelters, Shelter Bed Capacity, and Average Daily Occupancy, 1984 and 1988

	1984	1988	Percent Increase
Number of Shelters	1,900	5,400	190
Total Bed Capacity	100,000	275,000	180
Average Occupancy Per Night	70,000	180,000	155

U.S. Department of Housing & Urban Development, *The 1988 National Survey of Shelters for the Homeless*, March 1989.

These shelters serve what I will call the hard-core homeless. Our social workers estimate that 85 percent have been on the streets for a year or more, many have been homeless their entire adult lives or since they were deinstitutionalized years ago. More than half have disabling mental illness or are at least highly eccentric as to make conventional conversation impossible. Ninety percent or more abuse alcohol. Clinical depression is the norm. Although all are eligible for the basic general assistance or welfare grant of $154 per month, only a small fraction receive it. None of the mentally disabled receive the more generous Supplemental Security Income to which they would be entitled if they had housing.

We have doubled overnight shelter beds in Chicago since 1983 and opened additional warming centers on very cold nights. Still, 26 people died of exposure in winter 1987. In a similar minimal sense, this population's need for food is met through the 75 soup kitchens and 500 food pantries that operate in metropolitan Chicago, of which Catholic Charities supports seven kitchens and 50 pantries out of its own funds supplemented by federal and other governmental monies. No one, however, would say that this population has nutritional needs adequately met.

Intervention and Treatment

These minimal solutions, however, are totally inadequate from the standpoint of basic human dignity. Intervention, sheltered housing and treatment are needed to attack the underlying causes of the desperate and demeaning condition.

Short-term psychiatric hospitalization or detoxification, to which most of this population are periodically subject, should be followed by placement in residential programs offering services such as supervision of compliance with medication regimes, Alcoholics Anonymous meetings, psychotherapy and employment counseling. Unfortunately, halfway houses for the mentally ill are badly oversubscribed in Chicago. One such Catholic-run residential program in Chicago's Pilsen area, which served 360 individuals in fiscal year 1986, turned away 720 referrals in the same period. Thus, homeless mental hospital patients are routinely discharged to overnight shelters and the streets. The prospects for newly detoxified homeless alcoholics are equally bad, since there are only two long-term residential treatment programs for them in the city. Catholic Charities operates one of these, accommodating some 70 clients, for which the waiting list is typically 35 names long and the delay before admission three months.

The Second Stage

Additional "second stage" of long-term sheltered treatment programs are the key to making inroads into the entrenched homelessness of this population. Our 70 years' experience in the treatment of homeless alcoholics through such a program shows that modest success is possible. Likewise, those few community mental health centers that mount residential programs have succeeded in obtaining disability benefits or employment for mentally ill individuals and have established many in permanent living arrangements with ongoing outpatient support. But more of these programs are needed. In addition, very low-cost housing, such as was once supplied by the rapidly disappearing single room occupancy hotels, must be built to give permanent homes to rehabilitated hard-core homeless who are capable of only minimal employment or who must survive on disability benefits. . . .

The hard-core homeless are not the only homeless. Catholic institutions in Chicago operate 11 transitional shelters serving, variously, homeless families and individuals, pregnant women and women with children, battered women and their children, and runaway youth who have been victims of sexual exploitation. Catholic Charities directly operates five of these, three of which are geared primarily to serving families and individuals experiencing temporary crises. In fiscal 1986, 376 individuals lived in these three shelters for an average stay of 45 days, and there were 98 families among this group. In 1986 there were 1,603 requests for admission to these shelters, including 707 from families. Of these, we were able to accommodate only 170 or 10.6 percent of the total. The number of requests has grown at an average rate of 34 percent per year since 1980. This trend shows no sign of abating.

A Diverse Population

The case histories of persons served in these shelters demonstrates that homelessness affects people from very many walks of life. Unemployment or disability is nearly always a feature of their plight, but the deeper causes are varied, often complex and sometimes insoluble.

A Clear Need

The primary need of homeless people is shelter. *Why* people are on the streets is irrelevant to the need for shelter; and until people have shelter, attempts to address the many factors that may contribute to the need for shelter are premature.

The inability of existing shelters to meet the demand is clear. According to a survey of twenty-five cities, conducted by the U.S. Conference of Mayors, 24 percent of the demand for shelter was unmet in 1986; and shelters in eighteen cities had to turn people away because of lack of resources.

The cost of assuring minimal shelter is about $1.5 billion a year and should be borne primarily by the federal and state governments.

Kathleen Proch and Merlin A. Taber, *Public Welfare*, Spring 1987.

Often, all that is needed to stabilize a crisis situation is a little time and short-term casework. Consider the case of a 70-year-old woman who came to us destitute when the man for whom she had been keeping house died. She had a great deal of difficulty remembering much about her early life, so it took months to reconstruct her work history and qualify her for Social Security benefits. Only then could she obtain the housing necessary to apply for Supplemental Security Income. Here, the shelter played an essential role in achieving a successful outcome.

Most cases, however, don't end so satisfactorily. The underlying causes of homelessness are often much less tractable. Many times, the transitional shelters are asked to play roles for which they were never intended because the clients need to make transitions to rehabilitation or training programs and permanent housing situations that don't exist in adequate numbers.

Difficult Cases

Consider a personable young man of 26. Let's call him Ernie. Ernie has a high school diploma, but his IQ is about 80 or 90 and he is unskilled. He used to have a CETA [Comprehensive Employment Training Act] program job as a mail clerk, but his program funding ran out. Ernie gets general assistance of $154 per month and food stamps, but his rent runs him $165. To make ends meet, he must work. But we know that no one is going to hire Ernie for long. We know this because he volunteers at one of our foods pantries, and when he's given a list of five things to do he does the first two, but by the time he gets to the third he's forgotten what it is. Ernie lives on the edge of homelessness. He needs to make a transition to a sheltered workplace, but we can find no placement for him.

An even more difficult case is Mr. F, who immigrated to the United States 14 years ago. For years he lived with a family who gave him room and board in return for unskilled work in their family business. Mr. F and the family had a heated argument and the family took him to a community mental health center to be committed. The center's staff didn't see a need for hospitalization and released him to the street. He then obtained shelter with us. The caseworker assigned to Mr. F judged him to be developmentally disabled and encouraged him to apply for Supplemental Security Income, but he vehemently resented the implication of disability and refused. Neither would he pursue a general assistance grant; his pride would not permit it. He insisted that he was able to work and searched for a job for four months, but could not find one. Despondent, he left the shelter one day and never returned. There ought to be sheltered work and very low-cost housing for people like Mr. F. But these necessities are virtually unavailable in Chicago, and so Mr. F lives on the streets in misery and desperation.

Other cases I could relate would illustrate the need for literacy and basic skills training to solve cases of homelessness. While receiving these services, homeless clients need places to live—places other than transitional shelters. Longer-term "second stage" shelters should be created where people can stay while they acquire the skills necessary to become self-sufficient.

"The shelter system does little to reduce either the sources of homelessness or equip the homeless to achieve independence."

Shelters Are Ineffective

Charles Hoch and Robert A. Slayton

In the following viewpoint, Charles Hoch and Robert A. Slayton contend that shelters that provide too many services for the homeless teach them to be dependent on the system. They argue that the homeless need to learn to find housing for themselves, for example, rather than relying on a housing counselor to find it for them. According to Hoch and Slayton, if the homeless do not learn to be self-sufficient they will simply return to the shelter after every unsuccessful attempt to live independently. Hoch and Slayton based their conclusions on a study of single room occupancy hotels in Chicago, and wrote *New Homeless and Old: Community and the Skid Row Hotel*, from which this viewpoint is excerpted.

As you read, consider the following questions:

1. What is wrong with housing families in hotels, according to Hoch and Slayton?
2. How do efforts to maintain order in shelters undermine efforts to help the homeless, in the authors' opinion?
3. Why do Hoch and Slayton object to housing people with the same problems together?

Charles Hoch and Robert A. Slayton, *New Homeless and Old: Community and the Skid Row Hotel*. Philadelphia: Temple University Press, 1989. Reprinted by permission.

Caretakers and advocates for the homeless have prepared comprehensive plans that call for the provision of short-term emergency and transitional shelters combined with long-term low-rent housing. Comprehensive plans for solving the problem of homelessness acknowledge the danger of constructing only shelters to provide for the housing needs of the poor, and they usually propose a three-step program. The first is short-term care in shelters operated by the nonprofit religious and philanthropic organizations (although funded in part with government contributions) designed to meet the pressing needs of people facing day-to-day shelter uncertainty. Next is intermediate care in transitional housing, also operated by nonprofits with the purpose of aiding the homeless to get on their feet and back into the labor and housing markets. Finally, there is long-term shelter in low-rent housing made available to the homeless through government subsidy, enabling the working poor to maintain possession of decent and affordable housing. However, in most places all three steps are not being implemented. Emergency and transitional shelters have been created in response to compassionate appeals, but officials and the public are slow to take up the cause of affordable housing for the poor. This is a critical gap, however, in that arguments for such housing shift the focus from the homeless to the institutions that provide (or fail to provide) housing for low-income households. The first two steps in the plan assume that helping the homeless with shelter, services, counseling, and aid will enable them to reenter the marketplace successfully. Adopting the third step assumes that housing markets do not presently provide sufficient low-rent housing for the poor and that government funds should be used to do so.

Problems with the Plan

The three-tier plan offers the promise of a comprehensive and integrated housing strategy for the homeless. Unfortunately, the implementation of this plan in the context of fiscal retrenchment has tended to produce fragmented rather than integrated outcomes. Shelter schemes have received the bulk of financial support. The plan mistakenly treats short-term shelter provision as if such provision had been undertaken as the first step in a larger effort to provide affordable permanent housing for the poor. In fact, however, the proliferation of shelters reflects the continuation of a relatively unplanned emergency response to the homeless crisis.

The shelter response to the "new" homeless in urban areas usually followed two phases. Service providers and caretakers initially sheltered the homeless in existing SRO [single room occupancy]-type housing, especially SRO hotels. However, the diminished supply of SRO units soon proved inadequate, and local officials felt compelled to construct temporary and transitional shelters to fill the gap. Shelter providers gained public support for these shelterization policies by taking a compassionate approach to the problem that focused attention and treatment on homeless individuals. Thus, shelterization obtained public acceptance as a legitimate remedy for homelessness before the three-tier plan had even been proposed.

Spending Billions

Instead of attacking the causes of homelessness, we are spending billions of dollars on shelters. Building shelters, however, is like putting pots in the living room to catch dripping water without fixing the roof.

Todd Swanstrom, *The New York Times*, March 23, 1989.

Shelterization offers a poor substitute for the low-rent SRO-type housing it has come to replace, whether it be through the use of hotel vouchers or of shelter beds. For instance, the concentration of the dependent welfare families in SRO hotels designed for single people generates substantial overcrowding, enhances the mutual vulnerability of tenants, visibly publicizes the shame of homelessness, and escalates the cost of care without providing any means welfare families can use to secure independence. This shelterization of the SRO hotels is most poignantly illustrated by stories of welfare families in New York welfare hotels.

Promoting Dependency

The successful provision of emergency shelters has contributed to the shelterization problem as well. The number of shelters in urban areas has expanded rapidly since 1982, to the extent that the facilities now provide a system of specialized temporary accommodations for the homeless. The shelters successfully remove the homeless from the streets while meeting rudimentary human needs and, in so doing, promote the viability of shelterization as an acceptable (if inadequate) solution to the problem of homelessness. Caretakers use the vulnerabilities and pathologies of the homeless street people not only to inspire public concern and support for shelters but to assign the homeless to specialized shelters organized to meet particular needs. To provide professional care efficiently, caretakers concentrate homeless people who share a common weakness or debilitating condition. Paradoxically, sheltering the homeless in this fashion promotes the very dependency that shelter providers hope to help homeless clients overcome. Ultimately, the shelter system does little to reduce either the sources of homelessness or equip the homeless to achieve independence.

The perverse effects of shelterization derive, not from policy failures or inadequate funding, but from the widespread acceptance of shelters as an acceptable solution to homelessness. The moral arguments of liberals, which assert the moral worth of the homeless by emphasizing the vulnerabilities of homeless people, also tend to justify shelters as a legitimate form of treatment, rather than the dismal and demoralizing habitat of last resort they are. Caretakers and advocates, for example, overlook how the punitive caretaking practices needed to maintain order in a dormitory setting with a large number of strangers undermine efforts to offer compassionate counsel and attention. . . .

Lessons from the Past

Shelterization has long been the policy of local governments and local nonprofit caretaking institutions for the treatment of destitute homeless people. Dormitory shelters run by both private charities and government have long served as the housing of last resort for the poor in the United States. The most generous and extensive use of shelters was undertaken in the depths of the Depression. In the 1930s the federal government supported a shelterization policy that financed the expansion and operation of temporary shelters while legitimizing public responsibility for the shelter of the homeless across the nation. But federal involvement lasted for only two years (1933-35), after which funding reverted to state and local governments. Even with federal support, however, the shelters converted out of warehouses, offices, schools, and cheap hotels were described as little more than "thinly disguised flop houses" by Harry Hopkins, the director of the Federal Emergency Relief Administration. These perverse effects of shelterization became quickly apparent to shelter operators and residents alike, but these lessons were quickly forgotten. . . .

Some of the limitations of shelterization as a solution to the homeless problem become evident in an examination of the political disputes that have emerged over the size, quality, and location of shelters. The visibility and vulnerability of homeless street people, combined with the alarming growth in their numbers in the early 1980s, led local officials and caretakers who eventually acknowledged the problem to approve the speedy construction of emergency shelters that could accommodate large numbers of people. Advocates for the homeless, including both organizers and professionals, criticized the poor quality of these huge dormitories and insisted upon the provision of a broader range of services, longer stays, and greater privacy. The advocates urged dispersal of smaller shelters, but neighborhood residents resisted the location of shelters in their locale. What emerged in practice were two tiers of shelters: large dormitory short-term emergency shelters and smaller transitional long-term shelters.

The rationale justifying the provision of a two-tier shelter system combined the concept of vulnerability and the concept of moral desert. The less vulnerable homeless (e.g., single healthy males) are treated as less deserving and so tend to be channeled to temporary shelters, whereas the more vulnerable homeless (e.g., single women with children) are treated as more deserving and thus receive admission to the better quality transitional shelters. The classification of the homeless according to a hierarchy of needs tends to emphasize, however, only those vulnerabilities that caretakers are equipped to remedy. For instance, although most homeless people are unemployed, caretakers rarely treat this condition as a vulnerability by which to prioritize care, despite the fact that a lack of adequate earnings contributes profoundly to the social dependence of the homeless and their inability to rent a dwelling. Caretakers focus on physical handicaps, mental illness, inadequate education, or lack of training as the sorts of vulnerabilities they can help correct and so reduce the effect these have on the homelessness of their clients.

Creating Poverty

Investment in shelters is self-perpetuating. Shelter children—some of them only 14 years of age—are now becoming shelter parents. Shelter mothers, 28 years old, are now grandmothers. All of this creates a larger clientele for shelter organizers and provides a larger data base for shelter studies to be carried out by shelter experts.

While shelters remain a necessary first response to the requirements of aging alcoholics and psychotics living in our cities' streets, for most of the homeless they create a process that can only manufacture a much larger population of uneducated, unemployable, diseased and angry children who will grow into a destitute adulthood.

Jonathan Kozol, *The Washington Post National Weekly Edition*, April 17-23, 1989.

The transitional shelters attempt to create a sort of surrogate community among the homeless residents and staff, but a community that will prepare the clients to reenter both the labor and housing markets without the aid of other social ties. The concentration of a relatively small number of people (ten to twenty-five) with virtually identical needs makes the development of treatment programs and rule enforcement much easier for staff than if the clientele were more diverse. Though it encourages more efficient and humane treatment, such specialization of the shelter community may actually undermine efforts to foster practical autonomy on the part of the clients. Among the poor, achieving autonomy requires access to diverse social ties among class peers such as kin, friends, and neighbors, for unlike more prosperous members of our society, the poor cannot afford to purchase what they need to lead a private life. The independence of SRO residents is closely tied to mutual helping relationships with kin and friends outside the SRO world, as well as with neighbors and staff within it. These are precisely the sorts of ties that people sleeping in shelters or the streets have usually lost. Caretakers may expect their clients to take responsibility for reestablishing their independence, but since the resources and skills needed to make the transition are provided by the caretakers, these expectations ignore the sorts of community ties that the poor need to "make it" with so little income.

Contradictory Treatment

Shelters as different as the Catholic Charities Parish Shelter Program in Chicago and Jessie's House in a rural community of western Massachusetts . . . subscribe to the same contradictory principles of care: provide a supportive temporary environment while insisting that individual residents learn to become independent. The director of Jessie's House was quite candid when she explained that "the cooperative household is a demanding place to live. Guests must do their share of cooking, cleaning and childcare. They must respect the rights of others. And with the assistance of the housing advocate, they must begin to confront the causes of their homelessness and make progress toward finding a solution to their homelessness."

These organizational features place caretakers in the bind of treating and even creating dependence in the name of independence. Although many of the services provided are valuable to residents, they are no match for serious economic and social obstacles the residents face. Staff members usually acknowledge that their clients face an extraordinarily steep uphill struggle toward individual security but respond by providing more intensely and completely what they are equipped to provide. More caretaking, however, if the climb toward security is too steep, will simply result in backsliding. Most of those successfully aided during their previous bout with homelessness courageously struggle up the precipitous grade only to find themselves slipping down the slope of shelter security once again, and ending up at another shelter. Thus, as the size, quality, and locations of shelters become standard, the limitations that emerge are likely to become permanent institutional features unless we change the present policy of shelterization.

"We propose to get the most wretched, confused, and disruptive of the homeless off the streets and into clean and humane asylums."

The Homeless Mentally Ill Should Be Institutionalized

Charles Krauthammer

In the early 1960s a new means of helping the mentally ill was enacted. Known as deinstitutionalization, it was meant to allow the mentally ill to live outside of institutions with the help of community-based mental health centers where they could receive individual attention. Thousands were released, but the care centers were never developed. Some of those released wander the streets homeless. In the following viewpoint, Charles Krauthammer argues that building new asylums will relieve the suffering of homeless mentally ill people. Krauthammer is a senior editor for *The New Republic*, a weekly journal of opinion.

As you read, consider the following questions:

1. Why are the homeless mentally ill on the street, according to the author?
2. How does the sight of the homeless undermine society's morals, according to Krauthammer?

Charles Krauthammer, "How to Save the Homeless Mentally Ill," *The New Republic*, February 8, 1988. Reprinted by permission of THE NEW REPUBLIC, © 1988, The New Republic, Inc.

Hard cases make bad law. Joyce Brown is a hard case. She was one of the first persons locked up in Bellevue Hospital when New York City decided to begin sweeping the homeless mentally ill off the streets. And she was first to challenge in court her forcible hospitalization. She won, but an appeals court reversed the decision. Now a court has upheld her right to refuse treatment. The case, like Brown herself, is a muddle and making a muddle of the law. But it dramatically illustrates what is wrong with the current debate about the homeless mentally ill and with the limits of benevolence that our society permits itself to accord them.

Everything about Brown allows contradictory explanations. Court documents refer not to Joyce Brown but to Billie Boggs, the name of a local TV personality and one of the several false names Brown adopted. Is she delusional or did she choose new names the better to hide from her sisters who in the past had tried to get her hospitalized? She cut up and publicly urinated on paper money. Is that crazy or, as her lawyers claim, was she symbolically demonstrating disdain for the patronizing solicitude of strangers who gave her money? She shouted obscenities in the street. Is that the result of demented rage or was it her only effective means of warding off the busybodies of the city's Project HELP (Homeless Emergency Liaison Project) who might take her away to a hospital?

In sum, was she living on a grate at 2nd and East 65th because she is mentally ill or because she has chosen the life of a professional (her word) street person?

The Joyce Brown Puzzle

"A lucid and rational woman who is down on her luck," Brown's ACLU [American Civil Liberties Union] lawyer calls her. Being down on one's luck can just be that. But it can be a sign of something graver, namely the downward social mobility that is characteristic of schizophrenia and that is caused by the gradual disintegration of the personality that marks its course. The classic picture is: brilliant physics major drops out, becomes cabbie, becomes unemployed, drifts, becomes homeless. Brown was a secretary, lost her job, did drugs, wandered from sister's house to sister's house, then ended up a bag lady.

She is a puzzle. The first judge thought the ACLU's psychiatrists correct. The appeals court bought the city's diagnosis. Dr. Francine Cournos, the court-appointed (and thus disinterested) psychiatrist, determined that she did suffer from "a serious mental illness," that she "would benefit from medication," but that, since she refused, forcing it upon her would do more harm than good.

My guess is that Dr. Cournos is right. Brown most likely is a chronic schizophrenic. But that is a condition more reliably diagnosed by observing a patient's course than by a snapshot observation. The symptoms can remit for a time. When Brown was cleaned up, dressed up, and given attention, she appeared lucid and rational in court. Left on her own, however, her course had been relentlessly downhill. . . .

A Danger to Herself?

But the lawyers' duel was not just over whether Brown is mentally ill. Mental illness is a necessary, but not a sufficient, condition for involuntary commitment. The other condition is dangerousness: a person must also be a danger to himself or to others before he may be forcibly taken care of.

Meaningful Choices

The right to liberty has become an excuse for failing to address, even failing to recognize, the needs of the thousands of abandoned men and women we sweep by in our streets, in our parks, and in the train and bus stations where they gather for warmth. We have persuaded ourselves that it is better to ignore them—that we have an obligation to ignore them—because their autonomy would be endangered by our concern.

Meaningful autonomy does not consist merely in the ability to make choices for oneself. Witness the psychotic ex-patients on the streets, who withdraw into rarely used doorways, rigidly still for hours at a time, hoping, like chameleons on the forest floor, that immobility will help them fade into the grimy urban background, bringing safety and temporary peace from a world which they envision as a terrifying series of threats. Can the choices they make, limited as they are to the selection of a doorway for the day, be called a significant embodiment of human autonomy? Or is their behavior rather to be understood on the level of a simple reflex—autonomous only in a strictly formal sense? Far from impinging on their autonomy, treatment of such psychotics, even coercive treatment, of such psychotics, even coercive treatment, would not only hold out some hope of mitigating their condition but might simultaneously increase their capacity for more sophisticated autonomous choices.

Paul S. Appelbaum, *Commentary*, May 1987.

Brown's ACLU lawyers argued for the now traditional standard of dangerousness: imminent danger, meaning harm—suicide or extreme neglect leading to serious injury or death—within hours or days. The city was pushing for a broader standard: eventual danger, meaning that Brown's life was such that she inevitably would come to grief, even if it could not now be foreseen exactly when and how. Maureen McLeod, one of the city's lawyers, protested having "to wait until something happens to her. It is our duty to act before it is too late."

Is it? Generally speaking, the answer is no. We don't permit preventive detention even for criminals who we "know" are going to commit crimes. We have to wait and catch them. If involuntary commitment requires that dangerousness be shown, then it is not enough to say that something awful will happen eventually. By that standard, heavy smoking ought to be a criterion for commitment.

The city, trying desperately to stretch the dangerousness criterion to allow the forced hospitalization of Joyce Brown, had to resort to a very strained logic. After all, Brown had spent a year on the grate without any apparent physical harm from illness, malnutrition, or exposure. As the appeals court dissent pointed out, the city's case came down to a claim that Brown would ultimately be assaulted if she continued living and acting as provocatively as she was. But there is hardly a New Yorker who is not subject to assault merely by passing through the streets of New York. It is odd to blame the pathology of the city on her and lock her up to protect her from it.

Safe from Degradation

The idea of eventual harm as opposed to imminent harm is slippery and arbitrary. Brown had already been exposed to all the things that the city said would do her in—traffic, disease, strangers, the elements—and had survived quite nicely. The city was reduced to arguing that her luck was going to run out. It had to make this claim because it had to prove dangerousness. But why should a civilized society have to prove that a person's mental incapacity will lead to death before it is permitted to save that person? Should not degradation be reason enough?

The standard for the involuntary commitment of the homeless mentally ill is wrong. It should not be dangerousness but helplessness. We have a whole array of laws (e.g., on drug abuse and prostitution) that prohibit certain actions not primarily because they threaten life but because they degrade the person. In order to override the liberty of the severely mentally ill, one should not be forced to claim—as the city disingenuously claimed in the Brown case—that life is at stake, but that a minimal human dignity is at stake.

Joyce Brown is a tough case because it is at least possible that she is, in fact, not mentally ill at all, only unlucky, eccentric, and willful. Fine. But you cannot make that case for thousands of other homeless people. Helen Phillips, for example, picked up in the same New York City round-up as Brown, lives in Pennsylvania Station and is convinced that plutonium is poisoning the water. For the homeless who are clearly mentally ill, why should it be necessary to convince a judge that, left alone, they will die? The vast majority won't. It should be enough to convince a judge that, left alone, they will suffer.

Moreover, the suffering is needless. It can be mitigated by a society that summons the courage to give the homeless mentally ill adequate care, over their objections if need be. In a hospital they will at the very least get adequate clothing and shelter. And for some, medication will relieve the torment of waking dreams.

What prevents us from doing this is the misguided and pernicious civil libertarian impulse that holds liberty too sacred to be overridden for anything other than the preservation of life. For the severely mentally ill, however, liberty is not just an empty word but a cruel hoax. Free to do what? To defecate in one's pants? To wander around Grand Central Station begging for sustenance? To freeze to death in Central Park? The week that Joyce Brown won her reprieve from forced medication, three homeless men were found frozen dead in New York. What does freedom mean for a paranoid schizophrenic who is ruled by voices commanded by his persecutors and rattling around in his head?

What to do? The New York City sweep is only the first temporary step. It yields a bath, a check-up, a diagnosis, and the beginning of treatment. The sicker patients will need long-term custodial care in a psychiatric hospital. Others might respond to treatment and graduate to the less restrictive environment of a local clinic or group home. Many of these people will fall apart and have to be swept up and cycled through the system again.

A Danger to Themselves

We now have tens of thousands of demented people living on the streets, incapable of functioning normally, often posing some danger to themselves and others. But laws make it far too hard to commit people or to force them to get the treatment they plainly need. Civil libertarians defend their right to live this way, as if they were merely eccentric instead of deranged.

But letting a schizophrenic go untreated rather than abridge her liberty makes as much sense as letting a sleepwalker cross a busy street. Both, in some exotic sense, are acting of their own volition. Neither is capable of exercising the rational judgement required to preserve his well-being—or to avoid harming others.

Stephen Chapman, *The Washington Times*, March 31, 1989.

A sensible approach to the problem begins with the conviction that those helpless, homeless, and sick are the responsibility of the state. Society must be willing to assert control even if protection and treatment have to be given involuntarily. These people are owed asylum. Whether the asylums should be large or small, rural or urban is a matter for debate. (In my view a mix of asylum size and location would serve the widest spectrum of patients' needs.) What should by now be beyond debate is that the state must take responsibility for the homeless mentally ill. And that means asserting control over their lives at least during their most severe incapacity.

In 1963 President Kennedy helped launch the community mental health revolution that emptied America's state mental hospitals. Kennedy said in his message to Congress, "Reliance on the cold mercy of custodial isolation will be supplanted by the open warmth of community concern." It wasn't. In the turbulence of urban life even the mentally well have trouble finding community, let alone deriving from it any warmth. The mentally ill are even less likely to find it. Everyone is for community mental health care—until it comes to his community. This may be deplorable but it is a fact. And it is cruel to allow the mentally ill to suffer neglect pending rectification of that fact, under the assumption that until the community is ready to welcome the mentally ill, the street is better than the asylum. It is not.

In 1955 state psychiatric hospitals had 559,000 patients. Today there are about 130,000, a decline of 75 percent. Now, the incidence of severe mental illness has not changed. (Schizophrenia, for example, afflicts about one percent of the population.) Nor have drugs and modern treatment yielded a cure rate of 75 percent. Many of the 75 percent discharged from the state hospitals have simply been abandoned. They have become an army of grate-dwellers.

Rebuilding the Mental Hospitals

Helping them will require, first, rebuilding the mental hospital system. These hospitals do not have to be rural, they do not have to be massive, and they do not have to be run-down. The entire American medical care system runs on incentives. Psychiatry, social work, and nursing are not immune to the inducement that good money would offer to work with the severely ill.

Second, a new asylum system will require support for a string of less restrictive halfway environments and for the personnel to run them. New York State has announced a program to supply another element of psychiatric care: a new cadre of case workers to supervise intensively the most severely ill. They would follow the mentally ill through all parts of the system, even back onto the streets, and offer supervision, advice, and some services. But facilitators cannot be enough. If there are no beds in a state mental hospital when the patient is severely delusional or self-destructive, if there are no halfway houses during recovery or remission, then the case worker is left helpless. Anybody who has worked with the mentally ill knows that all the goodwill in the world is insufficient if the institutions are not there. Intensive case management can guide a patient through a rebuilt asylum system.

134

Without such a system, however, they can only provide the most superficial succor. The basic facts of the homeless mentally ill, destitution and degradation, will remain unchanged.

Rebuilding an asylum system is one problem we can and should throw money at. It will take a lot. The way to do it is to say to Americans: You are pained and offended by homelessness. We propose to get the most wretched, confused, and disruptive of the homeless off the streets and into clean and humane asylums. We need to pay for them. We propose capping the mortgage interest deduction: less of a tax break on your house so that others can be housed. (A cap at $20,000 would yield $1 billion of revenues annually.) A new asylum system begins with concern for the elementary dignity of the homeless mentally ill. But it does not end there. The rest of us need it too. Not just, as the cynics claim, for reasons of cleanliness, so that the comfortable bourgeois does not have his daily routine disturbed by wretchedness. Getting the homeless mentally ill off the streets is an exercise in morality, not aesthetics.

Choosing the Streets

Are the majority of the mentally ill, by whatever measure one chooses to apply, better off now than before the depopulation of the state hospitals? The inescapable answer is that they are not. . . .

Many of the mentally ill have drifted away entirely from any form of care. Given the freedom to choose, they have chosen to live on the streets; according to various estimates they comprise between 40 and 60 percent of homeless persons.

Paul S. Appelbaum, *Commentary*, May 1987.

It is not our aesthetic but our moral sensibilities that are most injured by the spectacle of homelessness. The city, with its army of grate-dwellers, is a school for callousness. One's natural instincts to help are suppressed every day. Moreover, they have to be suppressed if one is to function: there are simply too many homeless. Thirty years ago if you saw a person lying helpless on the street, you ran to help him. Now you step over him. You know that he is not an accident victim. He lives there. Trying to get him out of his cardboard house is not a simple act of mercy of which most people are quite capable. It is a major act of social work that only the professional and the saintly can be expected to undertake. To expect saintliness of the ordinary citizen is bad social policy. Further, to expose him hourly to a wretchedness far beyond his power to remedy is to make moral insensitivity a requirement of daily living. Society must not leave the ordinary citizen with no alternative between ignoring the homeless and playing Mother Teresa.

135

A civilized society ought to offer its people some communal act that lies somewhere in between, such as contributing to the public treasury to build an asylum system to care for these people. . . .

A new asylum system will not solve the homeless problem. Obviously the mentally ill are not the only category of homeless people in America. There are at least two others. Some of the homeless are not helpless but defiantly indigent. This is Joyce Brown, as she depicts herself: a professional street person, a lucid survivor who has chosen a life of drift. "It was my choice to live on the streets," she says. "It was an experience." Such people used to be called hoboes. Then there are the victims of economic calamity, such as family breakup or job loss. Often these are single mothers with children. Unlike the hoboes, they hate the street and want to get off, but lack the money, skills, and social supports. Some nonetheless try very hard: two homeless mothers who testified at a House hearing are actually working and putting kids through school.

We can debate for years what to do for these people. Should the hoboes who prefer street life be forced off the street in the name of order? And how best to help the homeless who are simply too poor to buy decent housing in the city? Whatever the answers to these questions, it is both cruel and dishonest to defer addressing the mentally ill homeless—for whom choice is not an issue and for whom poverty is a symptom, not the cause, of their misery—until we have figured out a solution to the rest.

Irrelevant Solutions

When the mentally ill infiltrate the ranks of another deviant group, criminals, we try to segregate them and treat them differently. We do not await a cure for psychopathy or a solution to criminality before applying different standards of treatment for the criminally insane. There is no reason to defer saving the homeless mentally ill until the solution to the rest of homelessness is found. Moreover, whatever solutions are eventually offered the non-mentally ill homeless, they will have little relevance to those who are mentally ill. Housing vouchers, counseling, and job training won't do much for Helen Phillips until we get the plutonium out of the water. And since we may never succeed, she will need more than housing vouchers, counseling, job training. She will need constant care.

The argument over how many of the homeless are mentally ill is endless. The estimates, which range from one-quarter to three-quarters, vary with method, definition, and ideology. But so what if even the lowest estimates are right? Even if treating the mentally ill does not end homelessness, how can that possibly justify not treating the tens, perhaps hundreds of thousands who would benefit from a partial solution?

"There is no need—either economic or therapeutic—for . . . large-scale institutions."

The Homeless Mentally Ill Should Not Be Institutionalized

Michael J. Dear and Jennifer R. Wolch

Michael J. Dear and Jennifer R. Wolch teach geography and urban and regional planning at the University of Southern California in Los Angeles. They are authors of the book *Landscapes of Despair: From Deinstitutionalization to Homelessness.* In the following viewpoint, they argue against proposals to build asylums for the mentally ill. Instead, they advocate helping the mentally ill find and keep homes. Community mental health clinics should be established to provide care for the mentally ill. The authors also believe communities should provide job training programs and social services. With these steps, Dear and Wolch maintain that the need for asylums would be eliminated.

As you read, consider the following questions:

1. Why is it unfair to say that the policy of releasing mental patients failed, according to the authors?
2. What do Dear and Wolch contend is the best way to care for the homeless?
3. What factors do the authors believe led to the release of patients from institutions?

Michael J. Dear and Jennifer R. Wolch, *Landscapes of Despair: From Deinstitutionalization to Homelessness.* Oxford: Basil Blackwell, Ltd., 1988. Copyright © Polity Press. Reprinted with permission of Basil Blackwell.

The history of American and Canadian social welfare policy reflects a slow but progressive absorption of state responsibility for programs devoted to the satisfaction of human needs and to the improvement of human welfare. These programs had hitherto been the responsibility of voluntary and charitable organizations. Very early in its history of intervention in welfare matters, the public sector developed an *institution-based* mode of response. This included lunatic asylums, hospitals, almshouses, orphanages and houses of industry. With the exception of the asylum, these institutions were usually located close to the heart of the urban population, where the need was greatest. However, the rural-based asylums were quickly engulfed by the spread of adjacent urban areas.

The institutions were destined to endure until well into the twentieth century. They acted as urban-based 'reservoirs' of disabled persons. During the 1960s, however, the release of the pent-up pressure in institutions was engineered via the 'deinstitutionalization' movement. Deinstitutionalization referred to the move away from large-scale institution-based care to small-scale community-based facilities. The movement assumed many particular manifestations, and incorporated widely diverse populations including the mentally disabled, the retarded, the dependent elderly, ex-offenders and substance abusers.

Deinstitutionalization

Overcrowded and essentially custodial institutions had increasingly come under attack for failing to provide adequate care and treatment and for the deplorable physical conditions that inmates were forced to endure. At the same time, a libertarian philosophy began to infiltrate the practice of social welfare. This philosophy was composed of two convictions: first, that prolonged institutionalization did more harm than good; and second, that it was an abuse of the civil rights of those who were subjected to it. As a result, in the 1950s several experiments were undertaken to demonstrate the utility of a noninstitution-based care. The most spectacular success was reported in the field of mental-health care, where programs designed to maintain patients in their homes showed the inappropriateness of a policy of universal hospitalization. The emergence of these new treatment philosophies coincided with the appearance of new chemotherapies for behavior disorders. This meant that the more acute symptoms of mental disorders could be controlled. Finally, a political and fiscal impetus in favor of deinstitutionalization arose. In the US for example, federal funds were made available to establish 'community mental health centers', with an explicit mandate to deliver grass-roots care at the local level. In addition, cash grant programs were extended to the disabled during this period, allowing individuals to be supported outside an institutional context. The federal programs were welcomed by many counties and states, which recognized that such funds would enable them to transfer a significant portion of the burden of care away from the state and county institutions, for which they had financial responsibility, to the community, which federal funds would support. In short, an unstoppable coalition of libertarian concern, treatment philosophy, chemotherapeutic advances, and politics and money came together almost by coincidence. The 'deinstitutionalization' movement had been born. . . .

The Homeless Crisis

A disturbing outcome of deinstitutionalization is the recent and widely publicized increase in the number of homeless mentally disabled. Definitions of homelessness itself vary; the condition is most simply defined as the absence of a stable residence, where one can sleep and receive mail. This is a relatively broad definition that would include living in a single-room occupancy unit (SRO) as equivalent to having a 'home'. Other definitions of homelessness emphasize the lack of shelter plus a dimension of disaffiliation or social isolation. Ellen Bassuk has drawn attention to the complexity of arriving at a simple definition by observing that: 'There is usually no single, simple reason for an individual's becoming homeless; rather homelessness is often the final stage in a lifelong series of crises and missed opportunities, the culmination of a gradual disengagement from supportive relationships and institutions.'

Still a Good Idea

It is vitally important that we provide help for the homeless, but there is no reason to retreat to institution-based care. Deinstitutionalization was, and is, a good idea. It argues that community-based care is better for the client, and that prolonged incarceration actually damages the chances for recovery—and infringes on clients' civil rights as well.

Michael J. Dear and Jennifer R. Wolch, *Los Angeles Times*, November 7, 1987.

The homeless population is notoriously 'fugitive' and thus difficult to count. National estimates for the US vary widely. A 1984 survey by the Department of Housing and Urban Development suggests that the most likely figure lies between 250,000 and 350,000 per night. This would imply that nightly demand for bed-spaces exceeds the supply by 140,000. These estimates have been severely criticized by human-service professionals. In contrast to the Department's low estimates, the National Coalition for the

Homeless puts the 1985 figure at 2.5 million homeless, up 0.5 million since 1982.

Most analysts agree that numbers of homeless have been increasing, largely due to an expansion in the homeless mentally disabled, thereby radically changing the composition of the homeless population. For years, the homeless population was typified by the familiar skid-row transient: male, alcoholic, averaging 50 years of age. Now young persons are found among the homeless, as well as women and families. The youthful population consists mainly of so-called 'chronic drifters', frequently diagnosed as schizophrenic or as suffering from affective and personality disorders and substance abuse, but who have never been institutionalized. L.L. Bachrach cites 'the existence of impoverished and highly stressed social networks, revolving-door utilization of the mental health service system, revolving-door involvement in the criminal justice system, high prevalence of physical illness, and high degree of resistance to traditional treatment interventions,' as characteristic of many homeless mentally disabled persons.

Media accounts reveal the extent to which the crisis of the homeless mentally disabled has reached into communities nationwide. In Boston, for example, most guests at homeless shelters are young (in their thirties) and have a history of mental illness. In St Louis, roughly half of the clients using homeless services were judged to be mentally disabled, showing symptoms of paranoid ideation and psychosis. A staggering 97 per cent of all guests at a homeless shelter in the Washington, DC area were found to suffer from some form of mental disability.

Increasing numbers of the homeless mentally disabled have had little or no contact with state hospitals or the ostensible 'safety net' of the community mental health system. Drastic cutbacks in public spending for social services and the absence of fully developed, coordinated and funded community-based programs for the chronically mentally disabled have exacerbated the crisis. . . .

No Need for Asylums

The deinstitutionalization movement can be regarded as the cumulative impact of a broad range of social changes that began in the 1950s. Its effect has been to create the most radical departure in human-services delivery since the first workhouses, prisons and asylums were built over 200 years ago. Under such circumstances, it seems somewhat churlish to criticize the advocates of deinstitutionalization for not planning the new welfare system properly. The many unanticipated and sometimes undesirable side-effects of deinstitutionalization could not have been foreseen without knowledge of later transformations in the social, political and economic climates. Moreover, despite the dilemmas facing community-based services, those early advocates took the first step in delivering what many had called for but which institution-based services had historically failed to provide: humane, caring support for the dependent. Thus deinstitutionalization was—and is—a necessary stage in the evolution of modern human services.

Defenseless Prey

Once invisibly warehoused, now sidestepped on sidewalks, the mentally ill are defenseless prey to the pendulum's swing. Says the Rev. Alice Callaghan, who for 15 years has run homeless centers in Los Angeles: "We've just been ricocheting between unacceptable answers." The better way, she and most experts believe, is smaller group homes with government-backed support.

Richard Stengel, *Time*, September 14, 1987.

On the other hand, reinstitutionalization is a step backward in our commitment to progressive service-support systems. We do not doubt that a small number of the service-dependent will always require a secluded, protected living situation; but there is no need—either economic or therapeutic—for such quarters to be provided in large-scale institutions. The onus should be on the advocates of reinstitutionalization to demonstrate the requirement for 'new asylums' and we are frankly pessimistic that such demonstrations can be made.

We believe that the earlier arguments in favor of deinstitutionalization retain their validity. So where do we go from here? What will the future look like?

Possible Futures

The future archeologist of human services is likely to discover one of two landscapes at the end of the twentieth century. The first is a *landscape of despair.* The perfect metaphor for this terrain is provided by the homeless who nightly populate the beaches of Santa Monica and Venice, California. They sleep next to the ocean at the continent's edge, a little distance from a tide that could sweep them away. This portrait of the landscape of despair presages the collapse of the human-service system and an abandonment of those in need. The lucky and resourceful who manage to survive hang on by their fingernails at the edge of society.

An alternative archeology is invoked by the many engravings of nineteenth-century asylums. These massive, isolated structures epitomized their creators' search for order, control and 'cure'. As Michel Foucault indicated, the asylum was only one episode in the history of haunted places. The future archeologist might discover a new *landscape of haunted places*, reflecting the rebirth

of the institution in the 1980s. The trend toward reinstitutionalization will again take the service-dependent out of sight and out of
mind. Only the ghosts of the incarcerated will be left to haunt
the community. And deinstitutionalization will be recognized as
but a brief respite in the history of the enduring institution.

Instead of these alternative archeologies, we call for a *landscape
of caring.* This is a landscape in which the potential and promise
of deinstitutionalization will be realized. In it, community-based
care is the norm: clients would have the right to service provision in their own community and communities would have the
obligation to look after their own.

Political Priorities

We recognize that political priorities of the restructured Welfare
State may stand in the way of the landscape of caring. First, there
is an acute *lack of political will* to deal with the problems associated
with the unfolding saga of deinstitutionalization. The various levels
of federal, state/provincial and municipal governments desperately
blame each other for every crisis. Such vertical conflict of interest
is further complicated by horizontal disputes among the various
sectors responsible for health, welfare and other key human services. When emergency or crisis situations cause a reallocation
of tax dollars, the funds often seem to be directed unimaginatively
toward buttressing the old institution-based solutions.

Secondly, the absence of political consensus derives partly from
the great *inertia in the health and welfare systems.* As we have
argued, deinstitutionalization has created a new apparatus of the
Welfare State. This has had two consequences. One is that competition over professional dominance and control has intensified
as the existing professional elites seek to protect their 'turf' from
the incursion of community-based counterparts. (The best example is perhaps the many union-based campaigns by psychiatric
hospital workers to persuade the public of the continuing need
for asylums and hence, for their jobs.) Another consequence is
that the diffusion of authority implied by community care has the
paradoxical effect of simultaneously extending and weakening the
traditional channels of social control. Doctors, psychiatrists and
social workers have penetrated as never before into the everyday
lives of individuals; yet the consequent stretching of the ties of
authority between professional and client has also meant that a
client group's traditional allegiance to one professional elite can
no longer be guaranteed. The rediscovery of the institution, in this
light, appears as a retrenchment which will once againt clarify
and consolidate professional control over the various client
populations.

Finally, the political reality of *community opposition* must be addressed. The recent history of deinstitutionalization has brought

more and more communities into direct contact with service-dependent groups which they had hitherto rarely encountered. Such communities are likely to be more resistant than previous opponents. Attacks by vigilante groups on the homeless even in traditionally accepting neighborhoods are further testimony to a groundswell of intolerance. The problem of opposition is unlikely to diminish. It may yet prove to be the tangential issue on which continued progress toward deinstitutionalization is blocked.

Shelter and Services

If these hurdles are to be overcome, how can we set about creating the landscape of caring? The general long-term objective must be to realize the community-based alternative promised by *deinstitutionalization.* This includes a full range of transitional living arrangements for the diverse service-dependent populations, as well as specific programs of care, social integration and employment.

In the short term, the immediate need is for *shelter and services.* For some clients, shelter alone will suffice; for others, ancillary support services will be necessary. Each new program effort should be accompanied by *community outreach.* Neighborhood support for deinstitutionalization must be mobilized; it is vital that neighbors feel willing, able, and—above all—legitimate in supporting community-based care. This can be achieved through tapping the deep roots of tolerance and humanity evidenced in most communities and by increasing neighborhood awareness of the problems of the service-dependent.

The Best Way

We cannot say that the idea of deinstitutionalization has not worked, because we never properly tried it. The best way to care for the homeless mentally ill is to deliver on deinstitutionalization's promise. This requires the provision of shelter and services through small-scale facilities in all communities.

Michael J. Dear and Jennifer R. Wolch, *Los Angeles Times*, November 7, 1987.

The simultaneous existence of tolerant and intolerant dimensions in a community psyche should not be regarded as an inexplicable contradiction. Our experience suggests that communities have generally favorable views of the *problem* of providing community care, but that they often reject the proposed *solution* for service delivery. Specifically, residents share a common concern for problems of the service-dependent, but have no wish to solve those problems in their neighborhood or on their block. A vital part of outreach is therefore a community education program to improve residents' understanding, familiarity and awareness of the problems of service delivery—and to suggest ways in which community participation can assist in overcoming these problems.

Service Hubs

One very practical way of proceeding on all these fronts is to develop *'service hubs'* throughout our communities. . . . This would involve identifying those neighborhood centers that already possess a reasonable standard of community and public transportation services; such centers could then be reinforced by the addition of necessary housing, services and employment opportunities. These decentralized hubs would have the effect of opening up a wide range of usable residential alternatives for the service-dependent. The amount of new support infrastructure would be minimal, since the hubs would already operate as independent centers of social interaction. Community opposition would be reduced if only small numbers of people and services were grafted onto an already diverse social fabric and pattern of land use and if all communities were perceived as sharing the 'burden' of caring. Perhaps the best example of a potential service hub is the suburban shopping mall, with its extensive range of services and often good transportation links. The introduction of a few extra housing units and a store-front community service center would transform the mall into another opportunity to build an effective community-based support system. . . .

If this or some equivalent solution is not adopted, we run the imminent risk of recreating the landscape of haunted places or a descent into the landscape of despair. In either case, the future archeologist will conclude that the lessons of history were overlooked.

Recognizing Stereotypes

A stereotype is an oversimplified or exaggerated description of people or things. Stereotyping can be favorable. However, most stereotyping tends to be highly uncomplimentary and, at times, degrading.

Stereotyping grows out of our prejudices. When we stereotype someone, we are prejudging him or her. Consider the following example: Ms. Jones believes that all homeless people are lazy and want a free ride from the government. The possibility that some homeless people are victims of economic and social policies and would work and establish a more settled life-style if jobs were available never occurs to her. She has prejudged all homeless people and will not recognize any possibility that is not consistent with her belief.

The following statements relate to the subject matter in this chapter. Consider each statement carefully. *Mark S for any statement that is an example of stereotyping. Mark N for any statement that is not an example of stereotyping. Mark U if you are undecided about any statement.*

If you are doing this activity as a member of a class or group, compare your answers with those of other class or group members.

S = *stereotype*
N = *not a stereotype*
U = *undecided*

1. Homeless people are crazy.

2. Government officials care only about keeping their jobs, not about whether they are helping people.

3. The number of homeless people is steadily increasing.

4. Mentally ill street people are a danger to normal citizens on the street.

5. Government welfare programs have helped a lot of people get through hard economic times.

6. Some street people are mentally ill.

7. Mentally ill people are better off on the streets because mental institutions are horrible, dehumanizing places.

8. Shelters provide emergency, temporary housing for the homeless.

9. Providing shelters for the homeless just affirms their lack of responsibility and initiative.

10. If street people didn't drink so much they'd be able to work and afford a home.

11. Many homeless persons use alcohol to numb the pain of their situation.

12. Government housing policies are grossly inadequate in meeting the needs of the poor.

13. People that run shelters for the homeless are all living saints.

14. Every person living on the streets today has been victimized by Republican fatcats in Washington.

15. A man who can't support his own family isn't much of a man.

16. Families without homes often live with relatives or friends.

17. Mentally ill people often need institutionalization to get well.

18. The government should do something to get the homeless off the streets so decent people don't have to see them.

19. Only a Democrat administration would care enough about the homeless to really help them.

20. Homeless children wouldn't *be* homeless if they had decent, loving parents.

Periodical Bibliography

The following articles have been selected to supplement the diverse views presented in this chapter.

Paul S. Appelbaum	"Crazy in the Streets," *Commentary*, May 1987.
Michael Dear	"Sleeping on Sidewalks Gets Rough When the City Can Steal Your Blanket," *Los Angeles Times*, July 1, 1988.
John Dillon	"A New Woe for Homeless on Skid Row: Hopelessness," *Los Angeles Times*, December 26, 1988.
Joan G. Evangelisti	"When Bob Died Homeless," *Newsweek*, October 3, 1988.
Theresa Funiciello	"Give Them Shelters," *The Nation*, April 2, 1988.
David Gelman	"Forcing the Mentally Ill to Get Help," *Newsweek*, November 9, 1987.
The Humanist	"Homelessness: A Humanist Response," May/June 1989.
Mickey Leland	"Toward a National Policy to End Homelessness," *America*, January 31, 1987.
Pia McKay	"I'm One of the Homeless—and Here's What I Think Should Be Done to Solve the Problem," *Glamour*, June 1988.
Dan McMurry	"Hard Living on Easy Street," *Chronicles*, August 1988. Available from The Rockford Institute, 934 N. Main St., Rockford, IL 61103.
Myron Magnet	"The Homeless," *Fortune*, November 23, 1987.
Tom Matthews	"What Can Be Done?" *Newsweek*, March 21, 1988.
Society	"Homeless Need More than Homes," March/April 1989.
Society	"Money, Medicine, and Homelessness," May/June 1989.
USA Today	"Homeless Need More than Shelter," May 1989.

Can Housing Policies Reduce Homelessness?

Chapter Preface

Because the homeless, by definition, do not have homes, it is not surprising that one of the most fertile debates surrounding the issue is housing.

Many solutions have been suggested for providing the homeless with homes. The people who support these measures argue that homelessness can be solved by a practical, no-nonsense approach: Allow the homeless to find homes, either with government vouchers, more public housing, or other measures. For every proposed solution, however, there are an equal number of people critical of it. The authors in the following chapter debate the solutions.

*"A comprehensive national housing policy ... is
needed to combat the housing crisis."*

A National Housing
Policy Would Help the
Homeless

John I. Gilderbloom and Richard P. Appelbaum

John I. Gilderbloom is an associate professor of urban policy at
the University of Louisville in Kentucky. Richard P. Appelbaum
is professor and chair of the department of sociology at the University of California, Santa Barbara. They are the authors of the book
Rethinking Rental Housing. In the following viewpoint, they argue
that only a new national housing policy can provide affordable
housing for the homeless. They recommend a housing policy
based on cooperatives, multifamily housing which is owned and
managed by the tenants.

As you read, consider the following questions:

1. What does the Houston example say about the free
   enterprise approach to housing, according to the authors?
2. Why do Gilderbloom and Appelbaum believe the free
   market is not truly free?
3. What is the authors' solution to the housing crisis?

John I. Gilderbloom and Richard P. Appelbaum, "Rethinking Rental Housing: A Progressive
Strategy," *Journal of Housing,* September/October 1989.

Housing the poor is one of the most serious domestic problems facing our country today. . . .

Between 1970 and 1983, median rents tripled, while renters' income barely doubled. Waiting lists for public housing have grown dramatically, forcing over two-thirds of the nation's cities to close off their lists to new applicants. These unfortunate conditions have been instrumental in creating an estimated million or more homeless persons in America—perhaps the greatest shame of the richest nation in the world. We believe that as our nation moves into the 1990s the crisis will only worsen.

The Houston Example

Conservatives blame government regulation in the form of planning, zoning and rent control as the major cause of this housing crisis. Yet, the experience of Houston—the much ballyhooed Free Enterprise City—seriously questions this assumption. Houston would appear to be ideal from the viewpoint of housing affordability. The city has an astounding 20 percent rental vacancy rate, little planning, no rent control, and lacks even zoning ordinances.

Yet, Houston nonetheless suffers from a serious housing affordability problem. The reality is that Houston's problems mirror those of the rest of the nation: a large homeless population, enormous waiting lists for public housing, half a million low- and moderate-income persons paying more than they can afford for housing, one-fourth of the low income population forced to live in overcrowded housing, and a zero vacancy rate for housing accessible to the disabled.

A study by the University of Houston's Center for Public Policy found that only 6 percent of qualifying low- and moderate-income people receive any form of governmental housing assistance. Despite this enormous housing emergency, thousands of rental units are demolished every year.

A Worsening Trend

Houston's wide-open approach to growth and development notwithstanding, Barton Smith, Senior Associate at the Center for Public Policy, has predicted that the problem of high housing costs will worsen in the coming decade, with rents doubling between 1988 and 1992. Clearly, the free enterprise approach Houston has taken has not worked. Nor will it work in other cities.

The truth is that the supposedly private rental housing market is far from free. Constraints exist not only in the form of local interventions (zoning, land use planning, rent controls, regulations on development, and so forth), but as exogenous interferences as well—the most significant of which include federal interest and tax policies, which are among the worst influences on local housing markets. . . .

151

Our research indicates that rental housing markets are far from competitive as is assumed, but rather embed significant institutional barriers to simple supply-side responses to changes in demand.

Among these barriers we would include mortgage interest rates whose fluctuations bear no relationship to local supply conditions; tax laws that encourage speculation; significant concentration of ownership and management of apartments; and government housing programs that treat housing not as a community good but as a commodity.

Filling the Gap

What is obviously needed is a Government housing program that helps fill the gap between what housing costs to build and manage and what poor and working-class consumers can afford to pay.

Peter Dreier and John Atlas, *The Progressive*, July 1989.

As a consequence, we concluded, policies aimed only at increasing housing supply will not necessarily result in lowered rents or prices. We argue, in fact, that neither the conventional market-driven response (build additional housing) nor its opposite (control rents) are likely, by themselves, to do much towards solving the rental housing crisis. We argue that government cannot rely on the "unregulated marketplace" to supply decent and affordable housing, any more than tenants can rely exclusively on rent controls.

Instead, we believe, a comprehensive national housing policy along the lines pioneered by Sweden is needed to combat the housing crisis. Such a policy would greatly expand the currently minuscule Third Stream of existing non-market housing [the other two streams being private ownership and rentals], to serve the increasing numbers of persons whose needs are not being met by the present system. . . .

Cooperatives with resale restrictions offer a useful example of attractive multifamily community-based housing, since they provide many of the guarantees ordinarily associated with home ownership. Such cooperatives are customarily operated through a democratically run, non-profit corporation which holds a single mortgage on the property.

Under a typical arrangement, each new owner purchases a share for a minimal down payment (for example, 10 percent of the value of the unit). Monthly payments then include each owner's portion of the common mortgage, plus a fee for maintenance and operating expenses.

When an owner wishes to move, he or she sells the share back to the cooperative, which then is resold to a new owner. Since the whole process takes place within the cooperative corporation, no new financing or real estate fees are ever involved.

Such cooperatives are termed *limited equity* both because the member's equity is limited to his or her share rather than the value of the unit itself, and because the appreciation in the value of that share is limited by common agreement to a low level. Cooperative members cannot sell their shares for what the market will bear.

In this way the sales price of units falls below the market price for comparable housing. While a typical home or condominium is sold and refinanced at ever-inflating prices many times over its life span, a limited equity cooperative is never sold.

The original mortgage is retained until it is fully paid off, at which time the monthly payments of the owners decrease to the amount necessary to operate and maintain the units. The principal difference between cooperative and private ownership is that within cooperatives, owners may change many times without the cooperative itself ever changing owners.

Owners share the full rights and privileges of private owners, including the tax benefits which are not available to tenants in rental housing. Ownership rests in the hands of residents, public agencies, or community organizations.

In all instances, management would be structured to promote resident involvement and encourage resident control over the use of space.

Numerous countries (Canada, Sweden, Finland, France, and Italy) have enacted programs to create cooperative housing. These actions have contributed to substantial decreases in the percentage of income paid into housing. The development of a sizeable cooperative housing sector could result in significant increases in affordable low- and moderate-income housing.

Tenants' Views

It would also result in greater control over the existing housing environment on the part of low-income residents, contributing to the "pride of place" often experienced by home owners. Ronald Lawson's survey of tenants in low-income housing cooperatives in New York City indicates that their level of satisfaction was quite high.

Tenants were almost unanimous in viewing their cooperative arrangements as preferable to—and less expensive than—rental housing. Many claimed that they were offered a sense of control that they had not previously known.

Many were saved from displacement by being afforded the opportunity to live in affordable cooperative units.

Tenants scored well, collectively, in basic indicators of effective management; experienced low vacancy rates and below-average turnover rates; and generally gave their cooperatives good marks on services provided. Moreover, the tenants stated overwhelmingly that they preferred cooperative living to private rental housing. . . .

Homesteading

When self-help rehabilitation is done the cost of bringing multi-family housing up to code can be 50 percent of the cost of conventional rehabilitation by private developers. Churches, poverty organizations, and nonprofits serving disadvantaged groups can sponsor non-profit housing development and rehabilitation. Abandoned and dilapidated units could be renovated by these organizations.

New York and Boston have been able to revitalize many declining neighborhoods by developing innovative homesteading programs. These programs result in greater housing opportunities for disadvantaged persons, an increase in tax revenue, more jobs, and the renewal of neighborhoods.

A statewide receivership program could be coupled with such programs, under which landlords who repeatedly refuse to fix code violations can be forced by the courts to cede rents for needed repairs (and, under certain circumstances, ownership of the unit as well).

Housing receivership programs have worked well in New Jersey. Poor neighborhoods could be dramatically turned around with the adoption of a large scale homesteading and receivership program.

New Measures

The private market alone cannot provide affordable housing for all citizens. . . . The conservative approach, based on encouraging free enterprise, has proven a failure in reaching those most in need.

On the other hand, the traditional liberal strategy of providing massive tax breaks and subsidies for builders and landlords has proven to be costly, inefficient, and largely ineffective as well.

New and bold measures, we believe, must be used to combat the housing crisis. We call for a new urban populist housing program where residents are empowered to develop their own solutions for the housing crisis. We believe that our Third-Stream housing program would go a long way towards providing decent and affordable housing in a humane and efficient fashion. Our program emphasizes local control, the benefits of ownership, and pride in community.

Providing for All

Paul Goodman wrote in *Growing Up Absurd* that "a man has only one life and if during it he has no great environment, no community, he has been irreparably robbed of a human right." Cities are judged great, not by the number of monumental buildings or people within their borders, but by their ability to provide justice and civility.

How well does the average American city address the needs of its citizens—whether they are rich or poor, black or white, old or young, able or disabled? Great cities are measured by the kinds of employment, housing, educational, aesthetic, and spiritual opportunities they afford their residents. All urbanites should live with dignity and without fear.

Great cities provide for all and exclude no one. By these standards—how many American cities would today be judged as great?

"The problem is not too few houses—rather, it is too much government."

A National Housing Policy Would Harm the Homeless

Joseph Mehrten

In the following viewpoint, Joseph Mehrten argues that people are homeless because current federal housing policies have made it too costly to build inexpensive housing for the poor. Zoning, building codes, and other forms of regulation, he contends, must be restricted if more low-cost housing is to be built. More federal government involvement in housing policy would only exacerbate the problem, he writes. Mehrten is a rancher, a businessman, and a free-lance writer.

As you read, consider the following questions:

1. What evidence does the author offer that regulations contribute to the homeless problem?
2. How does the lack of affordable housing affect children, according to Mehrten?
3. Why are land costs high, in the author's opinion?

Joseph Mehrten, "How to Sabotage the Homeless," *Conservative Digest*, May/June 1989.

Growing up in the country, remote from the services and cushions of the city, I early learned that actions have their consequences. More importantly, so do inactions: If wood isn't cut, you will get cold. If the barn roof isn't fixed, your hay will be ruined. If food isn't harvested and preserved for winter, you will get hungry.

So much for the cowboy primer in economics—except to add that if homes aren't built, they will not be available for habitation. The product of the equation is homeless people.

A Major Buzzword

No doubt you have noticed a proliferation of concern about "the homeless." It was a major buzzword during the 1988 election campaign. The subject is featured weekly on the tube and in the press. The homeless are visited and interviewed in abandoned cars, under bridges and in alleys from Portland to Atlanta. . . .

The homeless have been counted and recounted. They are blessed with help from government agencies, churches, compassionate people and philanthropic groups from coast to coast. Retiring U.S. Secretary of Housing and Urban Development [HUD] Samuel Pierce told a *New York Times* interviewer in January 1989, "What the studies have done so far is to put the number of the homeless at around 650,000 or below. A lot of people can use figures like two million to three million. Now where they get those figures is out of the air. There's no study, there's nothing, that will support that at all. We do know they're growing." . . .

The Problem

Homelessness is a much bigger problem around the world. As anybody who has traveled knows, much of the world outside of the U.S. is a slum. The United Nations Commission on Human Settlements has drafted a "Global Strategy for Shelter to the Year 2000" to help solve the worldwide housing crisis. (Of course jawboning and drafting by delegates, who spend more per employee on cocktail parties than perhaps any other institution, will not put up walls and roofs.) Nevertheless, the U.N. draft tells us: "Despite efforts of Governments and international organizations, more than 1 billion people have shelter unfit for habitation, and this number will expand dramatically unless determined measures are taken immediately." Surprisingly, the U.N. Commission admits that the private sector provides housing "more efficiently."

Thus, by comparison to the world, the United States is a housing paradise. However, if we keep emulating and adopting the Big Government philosophy that is endemic to most of the planet we could soon have a situation on a par with Romania or Ethiopia.

A recent addition to the long string of government housing failures was reported by AP on February 14th, 1989. "While 3,000 impoverished San Franciscans anxiously await a place to live, one out of every 12 of the city's public-housing apartments sits empty. . . . Apartments are littered with broken bottles and mirrors, splintered furniture and tattered curtains or are taken over by drug dealers who set up shop and are driven out when cocaine free-basing causes a fire. . . . The highest vacancy rate in San Francisco is among family apartments, which fluctuates between 10 and 25 percent. The housing authority loses $95,000 a month in lost rents as a result of vacancies."

Changes in Private Housing

I believe that the homeless advocates' prescription for solving the homeless crisis, which is essentially a massive federal construction program, will not make much of a dent in the homeless problem.

Certainly, the low-income housing crisis is very real. Of particular concern is the massive loss of Single Room Occupancy units in some cities during the 1970s. But while the housing crisis is one factor that lies behind the 1980s explosion of homelessness, it is rooted chiefly in changes in the private rental market. The low-income housing market has been decimated by such practices as condo and commercial conversion, rising rents, exclusionary zoning, and abandonment. The crisis is not, in my view, a result of the shift away from construction of additional public housing.

David Whitman, *The Heritage Lectures: Rethinking Policy on Homelessness*, 1989.

However, Big Government advocates are not satisfied with just a mess of their own. They are also messing in the private sector. There is widespread agreement among economists that rent control reduces the quantity and quality of available housing. This was demonstrated in a very enlightening study of fifty American cities done by William Tucker for the Manhattan and Cato Institutes. In the September 1987 *National Review* Tucker found:

"Truly widespread homelessness does not occur, however, until a city imposes rent control. At this point, all the people living in marginal circumstances suddenly find themselves confronting a 'housing shortage.' Because of the way the benefits and adversities of rent control are distributed, the poorest and least capable tenants usually find themselves bearing the brunt of its ill effects. This pushes homelessness to pathological levels—about two and a half times what it would be without rent control. . . . Although large numbers of tenants in the cities—perhaps even the majority—may reap some benefits, the adverse effects are being concentrated on a small but highly vulnerable minority. Unless these cities can be persuaded to give up rent control, the ranks of this minority—the homeless—will continue to grow."

In all the lather about the homeless, why is there no major-media concern about how government regulations are adding to the ranks of the homeless? Regulations surely deter the building of low-priced homes. One study, published by the Pacific Institute, indicated that California zoning restrictions, especially against suburban developments, raised the home prices some 60 percent above the U.S. average.

A young couple starting a family is forced to pay higher rent, for a longer time, then to pay a higher price when they ultimately buy. That is why it is difficult to own even though both parents are working. Children of families that are made less stable by economic pressures (like home shortages) are more prone to behavioral disorders. They are more easily seduced into deliquency, drugs, school failure, crime, and onto the street. Later, if they're lucky, these unfortunates may be rescued by people like those at Covenant House or the Door Of Hope.

The problem is not too few houses—rather, it is too much government. Indeed, the nationwide rental vacancy rate (8.6 percent) is the highest in two decades; the more than three million vacant rental units in the U.S. is the highest in our history. Irving Welfeld, author of *Where We Live* and a senior policy analyst at HUD, is quoted by columnist Warren Brookes: "'For every homeless person there are now 10 vacant year around units. The amount of crowding has also been sharply reduced. Fewer than 4 percent of the dwellings today have more than one person per room.' In fact, the average is now up to 2.2 rooms per person, the most generous living space in the free world. 'The last thing the federal government should do,' Welfeld told us, 'is to build still more housing. That would only make the housing glut worse, bankrupt thousands of small landlords, not to mention increase the insolvency of the thrift industry.'"

Being Up to Code

Sacramento developer Angelo Tsakopoulos remarks: "The government seems to have two conflicting attitudes—one that encourages building low-cost housing with tax incentives, low-interest loans and the like. And a second attitude that discourages the builder with permit costs and lengthy delays. This permit process alone, which can delay things for more than a year, adds at least 15 percent to the cost of housing."

He has found many officials to be very insensitive to housing needs. "When you talk to some EPA [Environmental Protection Agency] officials about how we need to build houses and factories and places to work for our people, they look at you like you are from Mars." Tsakopoulos also comments that, "Any society that doesn't provide for home ownership for its people will eventually collapse and go into revolution. People need to be educated to the benefits of home ownership. .... The new Secretary of Housing, Jack Kemp, recently told us that we need two million new housing units per year. It's not going to happen unless there is some abatement of regulatory obstacles."

Developers say that for every dollar in land costs for a building site, two dollars must be spent on the structure—otherwise the investment "will not pencil out." Land costs are high because there is a scarcity of buildable land. "Buildable" doesn't mean capable of holding a building. It means where building is allowed by the planners. The housing densities allowed by their zoning determines the number of "buildable" sites.

Ridiculous Regulations

"The artificial scarcity of buildable land is the biggest driving factor behind spiraling home costs," says California developer Bob Reeder. He continues: "Constraints on density are a three-to-five times greater factor in driving up home costs than is the permit process. It's the old law of supply and demand at work. And the planners have drastically limited the supply of land with low-density zoning."

No Real Difference

It should be clear that the housing and unemployment problems of the homeless are closely intertwined with the personal characteristics of the homeless. We need to address the problems of those individuals in a holistic manner and not simply think that changing macroeconomic policy or putting the federal government back into the building business would make a bit of difference to what we see on our streets.

Anna Kondratas, *The Heritage Lectures: Rethinking Policy on Homelessness*, 1989.

"I'm from the government," goes the old (bad) joke, "and I'm here to help you." Well, I'll never forget the building inspector who told me to spray herbicide on barely sprouting grass where in just a few days it would be under the floor of a new house. These are usually good people just doing their job, but they almost totally control building in this country with the Uniform Building Code. Innovation without costly engineering is almost impossible. The typical response of government-built slums is not the answer. Requiring Environmental Impact Reports covering ridiculous minutiae generate huge additional costs that are ultimately borne by the home consumer. Legislators, if they are really concerned about the growing number of families in our environment who can't afford decent housing, should push for deregulation in the home-building industry.

"If homelessness is going to go, rent control is going to have to go first."

Abolishing Rent Control Would Reduce Homelessness

William Tucker

In the 1970s, rent control—a cap on the amount that rents could increase—was introduced in many cities in the hopes of providing more affordable housing. But the unexpected effect of rent control, according to William Tucker, was to promote homelessness by causing a shortage of low-income housing for the poor. Artificially low rents cut into landlords' profits, thus keeping them from constructing inexpensive housing for the poor, he writes. William Tucker is the New York correspondent for *The American Spectator*, a monthly magazine.

As you read, consider the following questions:

1. According to Tucker, what is wrong with the usual explanations of homelessness?
2. How does the author believe rent control affects vacancy rates?
3. Who does rent control help, according to Tucker?

William Tucker, "America's Homeless: Victims of Rent Control," The Heritage Foundation *Backgrounder*, January 12, 1989. Reprinted by permission.

America's housing situation poses a strange paradox. Overall, Americans have never been better housed. The rental vacancy rates for 1987 stood at 8.5 percent, the highest in two decades. More than 60 percent of Americans live in their own homes. And as Rutgers University scholars George Sternlieb and James W. Hughes of the Center of Urban Policy Research point out, there is now one bedroom for every American.

Yet in the midst of this plenty, city after city appears to suffer from a housing shortage. Worse still, homelessness has emerged as a national issue. In Los Angeles, vagrants sleep under bridges, on park benches, in vacant lots. In New York City, homeless beggars and panhandlers have swelled to such numbers that Mayor Edward Koch officially advises residents and visitors not to give them money.

How did America arrive at such pockets of poverty in the midst of plenty? There are many contributing factors. The release of several hundred thousand mental patients over the past two decades obviously has created a hard core of "street people" literally incapable of caring for themselves. Illegal immigration in Florida and the Southwest probably has fed homelessness in those areas. High unemployment may have caused some problems in hard-hit cities like Detroit and Houston. And there is no question that cutting back Social Security benefits for the disabled left a small but identifiable group of Americans with little or no personal resources.

Inadequate Explanations

Nevertheless, all these explanations fall short of a complete or satisfying explanation of the problem in the cities. The best estimates are that former mental patients constitute no more than one-third of the homeless in most cities. High unemployment seemed like a plausible explanation in the early 1980s, but jobless rates are now at a fifteen-year low and still homelessness persists. Poverty rates also have fallen, yet the homeless remain.

Another widely touted explanation—the Reagan Administration's cutback in construction of public housing—can be dismissed out of hand. Proponents of this theory cite the sharp reductions in the authorization of new units after 1981. On the face, these figures seem compelling.

But the argument overlooks the fact that public housing units can take five to ten years to complete after they have been authorized by Congress. (Some units in the pipeline, in fact, date from the Ford Administration.) The number of federal public housing units actually completed over the last decade gives a very different picture.

In fact, the 1980s have been boom years for public housing. Yet this upswing coincides with the emergence of large homeless populations.

Thus, analysts who hunt for failures of government largesse as the cause of homelessness are looking in the wrong direction. What they fail to see is that housing is actually one of the most highly regulated industries in the country. These regulations are not imposed at the federal or state level, but at the local level, where the narrow interests of local residents often block the market's ability to provide housing. These impediments to housing usually take two forms—rent control and exclusionary zoning regulations.

Since the 1970s, commentators have been arguing that exclusionary zoning was limiting the housing options for the poor. Most of these negative incentives remain in place today. But by far the biggest impediment to low-income housing has been rent control. Over 200 communities, including nearly all the major cities on the East and West Coasts, block rent increases. These cities now all suffer serious homeless problems. An analysis of the rates of homelessness in 50 major cities across the country shows that rent control is the only factor that is associated with high rates of homelessness. The commonly suggested explanations—high unemployment, high poverty rates, lack of public housing—show no correlation.

An Unfair System

Rent control has visibly aggravated homelessness and can only be expected to do worse in the future. . . .

The New York City experience has proven that the greatest benefits of rent control accrue to the affluent. All the great bargains in New York are concentrated in posh areas of Manhattan, on the Upper East and Upper West Sides and in Greenwich Village. The resulting housing shortage, on the other hand, is experienced most acutely by people on the margins—growing families and the poor. They are the ones who become homeless. If this is a system you are willing to support, you are welcome to it. To my mind, it just isn't fair.

William Tucker, *The Progressive*, July 1989.

Rent control blocks the workings of the housing market and discourages developers from responding to increases in demand for low-income housing. Moreover, rent control often goes hand-in-hand with other anti-growth restrictions, such as zoning and building moratoria. All these market interventions tend to benefit existing homeowners and current residents, but create significant disadvantages for newcomers and the poor.

A permanent solution to the homeless problem will require the federal government to encourage cities to clear a path through the tangle of local regulations that restrict the supply of low-income housing. It will mean finding ways to discourage local municipalities from using zoning and growth controls as a cost-free way of improving local property values at the expense of out-siders seeking housing.

Most of all, it will mean overturning municipal rent control. Although generally tolerated as a legitimate "police power," rent control is in truth nothing but an attempt by sitting tenants to shift their housing costs to outsiders and future tenants. Although it produces some short-term benefits for some individuals, the long-term effect is to make housing more scarce and expensive for everybody. If homelessness is going to go, rent control is going to have to go first. . . .

Disputed Numbers

In 1986, with the help of New York's Manhattan Institute for Public Policy, and the Cato Institute in Washington, D.C., the author undertook a lengthy statistical analysis to try to determine what is causing homelessness. The data base was the statistics compiled from 40 major cities in the 1984 *Report to the Secretary of Housing and Urban Development on the Homeless and Emergency Shelters.* The HUD numbers have been disputed. Homeless advocates dismiss them because HUD estimated the national homeless population at 350,000 for 1983-1984, whereas activists insist that the number is 2 million to 3 million. On the other hand, subsequent studies involving actual head counts of the homeless have provided strong evidence that the HUD numbers were approximately correct or even overestimated the problem. In fact, HUD's figures for the homeless population in several cities exceeded the estimates made by the homeless advocates who so bitterly attacked the federal study. Yet as a means of comparing homeless populations between cities, the HUD report is a legitimate starting point. Since HUD used the same counting methods from city to city, it can be assumed that the estimates at least maintain some proportional accuracy.

Regression analysis was used to measure the correlation between per capita homelessness in each city and such independent variables as: 1) the size of the city, 2) local unemployment rates, 3) local poverty rates, 4) the availability of public housing, 5) the percentage of population growth or loss over the past fifteen years, 6) the average annual temperature, 7) average annual rainfall, 8) rental vacancy rates, and 9) the presence or absence of rent control. . . .

Surprisingly, the regression of homeless figures against factors commonly assumed to influence homelessness—unemployment, poverty, availability of public housing—uncovered no significant correlations. Rainfall had no effect, but average annual temperature showed a small correlation. Warmer cities have slightly more homelessness—about 3 percent for every one degree increase in temperature. This might suggest that people find it easier to be homeless in warmer climates, or it could imply—as Sunbelt politicians have often charged—that there has been some migration of the homeless to warmer climates.

The Cause of the Shortage

Truly widespread homelessness does not occur until a city imposes rent control. At this point, all the people living in marginal circumstances suddenly find themselves confronting a "housing shortage." Because of the way the benefits and adversities of rent control are distributed, the poorest and least capable tenants usually find themselves bearing the brunt of its ill effects. This pushes homelessness to pathological levels—about two and a half times what it would be without rent control.

Wlliam Tucker, *National Review*, September 25, 1987.

City size was examined to test the hypothesis that bigger cities attract the homeless. There is no correlation. Population growth also was examined, on the theory that homelessness develops because the housing industry is unable to keep pace with a rapid in-migration. In fact, the growth factor produces a slightly negative correlation—older, shrinking cities tend to have slightly higher rates of homelessness, suggesting perhaps that the problem has to do more with the decay of cities than with their expansion.

The housing vacancy rate correlates fairly strongly with the rate of homelessness. The coefficient is .387; meaning that vacancy rates account for about 15 percent of the variations in homeless rates between cities. As would be expected, those cities with lower vacancy rates have more homelessness. This clearly suggests that at least some of the problem is related to housing availability, as well as individual pathology.

The Link

The most remarkable correlation is with rent control. By itself, rent control accounts for 27 percent of the variation between cities. The certainty of such correlations is measured by what statisticians call the "P-factor." In the case of rent control this was below .01—about as certain as a social correlation ever gets. (In the social sciences, a P-factor below .1 usually indicates statistical significance.) When combined with the temperature factor, rent control explains about 31 percent of the variation between cities.

Running the various factors simultaneously produces one more surprising revelation. When rent control and vacancy rates are combined, the vacancy rate disappears altogether as a significant factor in homelessness. This means that the only significant factor relating to vacancy rates is the difference between cities with and without rent control. When vacancy figures are considered separately, the reason becomes clear. The nine rent-controlled cities studied had the nine lowest vacancy rates in the country.

Among the 41 cities without rent control, only Worcester had a vacancy rate under 4 percent, while all nine rent-controlled cities had vacancy rates below 3 percent. The wide variation in vacancy rates among other non-rent-controlled cities—from 4 percent in Philadelphia to 18 percent in New Orleans—has no impact on homelessness and seems to reflect only normal market fluctuations. Only in cities with rent control are vacancy rates consistently low.

Regression analysis, of course, cannot prove cause and effect. It only measures correlations. It could be argued, therefore, that low vacancy rates have caused cities to adopt rent control, rather than the reverse. But the rental history of all nine cities with rent control tells a different story. New York City, which has extended the rent controls first enacted in 1943, had an 8 percent vacancy rate in 1941: since then, the rate has never risen above 3 percent to 4 percent.

A Clear Pattern

The other cities adopted rent control during the 1970s as a response to inflation—not housing shortages. Both Newark and Boston adopted rent control as an extension of Richard Nixon's 1971 wage and price controls. In 1980, vacancies were still a normal 6 percent, but have since dropped below 3 percent. Most California cities adopted rent control after 1977, when anti-tax advocate Howard Jarvis unwisely promised tenants that the property tax limitations of Proposition 13 would lead to rent reductions. When these reductions failed to materialize, a wave of anti-landlord agitation led to a dozen cities adopting rent regulation. Half of all California tenants now live under rent control. The results have been the same whenever controls have been put in place. In 1980, both Santa Monica and Berkeley had normal vacancy rates of about 6 percent. Their draconian rent control ordinances—generally considered the strictest in the country—have since driven vacancies to below 2 percent.

Thus, rent control appears to explain why certain major cities on the East and West Coasts—Boston, New York, Washington, Los Angeles, and San Francisco—have experienced inordinately high homeless populations in recent years. The pattern emerging from the statistics is clear: the worst homelessness is concentrated in those few cities with rent control. . . .

Experience has shown tenants who do best under rent control

166

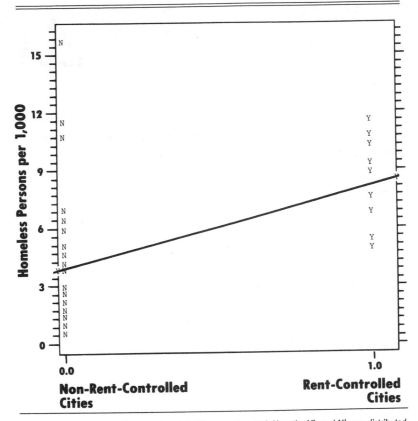

Y's here and throughout indicate rent control; N's, no rent control. Here the Y's and N's are distributed on the extremes of the horizontal axis because Rent Control=1 and No Rent Control=0. The important point to note is the relative vertical distributions of the two groups.

are longstanding incumbents who can expect to remain in their apartments for many years. Senior citizens and couples with small families (who tend to be affluent) do well. Those who do poorly are people who must change jobs often, and couples with growing families. Once established in their privileged positions, rent-controlled tenants can become a powerful political force against any new development. . . .

To solve the housing shortage, America's poor must be given an opportunity, as consumers, to take part in the housing market. . . . Middle-class rent-controlled tenants will have to give up some of the benefits they enjoy at the expense of the poor. There is no other way in which the crisis of homelessness can be solved.

"The case against rent control is a fraud: Rent control is a scapegoat for the nation's housing ills."

Abolishing Rent Control Would Not Reduce Homelessness

John Atlas and Peter Dreier

John Atlas is president of the National Housing Institute, a New Jersey-based organization which provides training for tenant groups. Peter Dreier is the director of housing for the Boston Redevelopment Authority. In the following viewpoint, they argue that rent control prevents homelessness rather than increasing it. Rent control helps save the poor, the elderly, and families with children an average of $100 a month, they argue.

As you read, consider the following questions:

1. Why is rent control under attack, according to the authors?
2. What evidence do Atlas and Dreier present that rent control prevents homelessness?
3. Why are the authors against limiting housing assistance to the poor?

John Atlas and Peter Dreier, "The Phony Case Against Rent Control," *The Progressive*, April 1989. Reprinted by permission from *The Progressive*, 409 East Main Street, Madison, WI 53703.

The nation's housing crisis is a manageable problem. It is simply a matter of national priorities. In 1980, for every dollar spent on housing, the Federal Government spent $7 on the military. By 1988, for every housing dollar, Washington spent more than $40 on the military. Federal housing policy needs a major overhaul, based on the premise that decent affordable housing is a basic right.

Today, among the most urgent tasks are to defend rent control and to promote the construction of affordable housing for poor and working-class families.

The National Coalition for the Homeless estimates the homeless population at between two and three million. An increasing percentage of these are families and the working poor who simply can't afford housing on their low wages. Workers near the poverty line are now paying more than half of their limited incomes just to keep a roof over their heads. The only roof that many can find is over a vacant building, or an abandoned car, or an emergency shelter.

"Homelessness is a national tragedy of appalling proportions," said Jack Kemp, George Bush's Secretary of Housing and Urban Development, at his confirmation hearings. But if Kemp pursues the right-wing agenda on housing, he will only deepen that tragedy.

Housing advocates hope that Kemp, who probably harbors greater political ambitions, will take a pragmatic rather than an ideological approach as a way of building a constituency among the poor, the housing industry, and big-city mayors. One early test of Kemp's thinking will be his response to pressure from the real-estate industry, right-wing think tanks, and conservatives in Congress who are waging a holy war against rent control.

Across the country, rents are skyrocketing. According to a study by the Harvard Center for Housing Studies, rents are now at their highest level in two decades. Tenants are intensifying their demands for rent control, but the basic premise of rent control is under assault by right-wingers and their allies.

A Fraudulent Case

What's behind this new attack on rent control? For landlords, it's a simple matter of greed. While studies demonstrate that rent control allows apartment owners a reasonable profit, it does limit unbridled rent-gouging and real-estate speculation. For New Right thinkers, the battle is part of the larger ideological assault on regulation of the private sector; they view rent control as both an unwarranted interference with private-property rights and a misguided effort to preserve affordable housing. And for some politicians, opposition to rent control is an easy—if obvious—way to curry favor with campaign contributors from the real-estate industry and win plaudits from conservative opinion-leaders.

But the case against rent control is a fraud: Rent control is a scapegoat for the nation's housing ills and for the failure of free-market housing policy.

Rent control has helped slow down gentrification, curb displacement of poor and working-class families, and minimize the disruption of neighborhoods that otherwise would have collapsed under the pressure of free-market forces. In housing, the invisible hand often carries an eviction notice.

Tucker's Study

The Heritage Foundation claims that rent control actually causes homelessness. In a study prepared by right-wing journalist William Tucker, the Heritage Foundation purported to show that rent control makes housing "more scarce and expensive for everybody."

Tucker looked at fifty cities and found that seven out of nine with rent control also have the largest homeless populations. The fact that forty-one of the cities with sizable homeless problems did *not* have rent control—proving that rent control doesn't cause homelessness—didn't bother Tucker. He noticed a strong correlation between low vacancy rates and rent control. "A 1 per cent decline in the vacancy rate was roughly associated with a 10 per cent increase in homelessness," he said. By some twisted logic, he then concluded that rent control causes homelessness.

One Available Tool

Until Washington renews its responsibility to help house poor and working-class people, rent control will be needed as the one tool available to local governments to help such people keep a roof over their heads.

Peter Dreier and John Atlas, *The Progressive*, July 1989.

In fact, the reverse is true. When there is a severe housing shortage and low vacancy rates, rents begin to escalate. Low-income tenants get pushed into the streets and shelters. Those tenants who can hold on start to push for rent control.

Arguing that rent control causes homelessness is like arguing that the sun comes up because the rooster crows. Tucker concedes that his analysis "cannot prove cause and effect"—it can only demonstrate coincidence. But, he claims, "once correlations have been discovered, however, we can *theorize* about what the causal connections might be."

Despite the obvious holes in Tucker's theorizing, he has become an intellectual stalking horse for the Right. Though he had demonstrated no prior expertise in housing policy, his initial study of rent control was funded by the libertarian Cato Institute and housed at the Manhattan Institute, another right-wing think tank that sponsored Charles Murray, whose *Losing Ground* attacked welfare as the cause of poverty.

Tucker has sold himself as a housing expert, and his articles have appeared in *The American Spectator, The Wall Street Journal,* and *The New Republic,* on the cover of William Buckley's *National Review,* and on the op-ed pages of *The New York Times.*

He is a clever propagandist. In an article in *New York* magazine, he offered readers $50 to send in examples of "rich and famous" New Yorkers living in rent-controlled apartments. When Morton Downey Jr. did a show on rent control, he invited Tucker, who dutifully bashed tenant activists. Just a few days before Bush announced his choice of Kemp for Housing and Urban Development, the Heritage Foundation called a press conference and brought Tucker to the podium to remind the audience that the thousands of New Yorkers sleeping on grates and in shelters only had rent control (and its liberal proponents) to blame.

The Media Blitz

Tucker and the Right have made headway in their attack. Twice since 1987, *The New York Times* has run editorials opposing rent control. One of these, attacking Governor Mario Cuomo's plan to retain rent control, was headlined MR. CUOMO PROMOTES HOUSING CRISIS.

And in May of 1988, conservative Senator William Armstrong, Republican of Colorado, added a last-minute amendment to the bill reauthorizing McKinney Act funds for the homeless. Armstrong's measure required HUD to study how rent-control laws might be causing homelessness. The amendment passed.

About 200 cities—including New York, Boston, Los Angeles, Washington, and San Francisco—have adopted some form of rent control. Conservatives are hoping that Jack Kemp will withhold Federal housing funds from these municipalities until they eliminate rent control.

The Evidence of Experience

Most people, using common sense, recognize that rent control helps *prevent* homelessness. In fact, the arguments against rent control crumble when confronted with evidence based on experience.

Rent control has had no adverse impact on new construction, housing maintenance, abandonment, or property taxes, conclude two social scientists, Richard Appelbaum of the University of California and John Gilderbloom of the University of Louisville, in their book, *Rethinking Rental Housing.*

For example, in New Jersey, which has about half of all cities in the country with rent control, developers continue to build as many apartments in communities with rent control as in communities without it. Indeed, Appelbaum and Gilderbloom have shown that some cities with rent control actually outpaced those without in the construction of new apartments.

A study of local rent control conducted by the Urban Institute to evaluate the program in Washington, D.C., found that rent-control policy primarily benefited the elderly, the poor, and families with children, typically saving households $100 a month. Rent control in Washington was found to have little impact on new construction, repairs, or housing values.

A Fundamental Right

Affordable housing should not be a privilege to be doled out by the wealthy. It is a fundamental human right. Protecting rent control and tenants' rights is a crucial component of any effort to solve the homeless crisis and create more affordable housing.

Chuck Idelson, *People's Daily World*, August 27, 1988.

Most local rent-control laws exempt all newly constructed housing, guarantee a fair and reasonable return on investment, and allow annual rent increases as necessary to cover increases in operating costs. Rent control simply limits extreme rent increases where landlords can otherwise take advantage of tight housing markets. And any builder will confirm that the volume of new apartment construction depends less on rent control than on land prices, zoning laws, changes in interest rates, the income and employment of an area, and the availability of Government housing subsidies.

Capping Deductions

Still, some neoliberals claim that housing assistance, like Social Security, should be limited to the poor to make it more efficient and equitable; in other words, they favor a means test. But programs that serve only the poor are demeaning and often less efficient, requiring an added bureaucracy to check for cheats and, more importantly, to undercut broad public support for the program itself. Compare Medicare for the middle class with Medicaid for the poor.

In New York City, such critics as William Tucker complain that rent control helps Mia Farrow, Ed Koch, and other affluent tenants. But even in New York City, most tenants pay more than they can afford: 70 per cent of all renters have household incomes of less than $25,000 a year.

Rent control was not designed to be a welfare program but a consumer-protection policy. Appelbaum and Gilderbloom demonstrate that despite the diversity of apartment ownership in many cities, landlords operate as a monopoly, setting price levels through networks such as real-estate boards. In that way, they resemble a local gas or electric utility. And no one asks government utility boards to regulate the price of gas and electricity only for low-income consumers.

Those who attack rent control because it assists the wealthy along with the poor should logically favor Federal housing entitlements for low-income tenants and a beefed-up Federally subsidized housing-production program. But that would cost billions of Federal dollars and probably require a tax increase on the rich—policies conservatives and neoliberals don't like.

And if fairness is the overriding issue, the Government should cap the home-owner tax deductions for mortgage interest and property taxes so that they primarily help poor and working-class families, not the wealthy, whom they currently favor. These deductions cost the Federal Government more than $35 billion in 1988—four times the HUD budget. About $8 billion of that went to the 2 per cent of taxpayers who earn more than $100,000—with a bonus for those with two expensive homes. Most home owners benefit minimally from such deductions; half do not claim them at all. Tenants, of course, whose incomes are on average half that of home owners, are not eligible. . . .

A Progressive Program

Where are we now? Unfortunately, the political conditions do not exist to guarantee that every American has decent and affordable housing. Bush and Congress are in no mood to make additional expenditures. To free up the money, Congress would have to cut the military budget and increase taxes on big business and the wealthy, neither of which seems likely.

Yet, public-opinion polls sponsored by the National Housing Institute and other groups reveal widespread support for a renewed national housing program and even for tax increases to pay for such a program. This sentiment must be transformed into political support before specific legislation can be enacted. . . .

A comprehensive progressive housing program is unlikely to get serious attention in Congress so long as progressive forces are fragmented and isolated. The strategic question is what housing agenda is both politically possible and progressive—a stepping stone toward more fundamental reform.

At the moment, a key strategy must be to defend rent control. On its own, it can't solve the housing crisis; it is, simply, one tool available to local government to deal with astronomical rents and a shortage created in Washington. But rent control can enable large numbers of poor and working Americans to have a roof over their heads. That is the least we can do.

"Squatting efforts are both increasingly common and justified."

The Homeless Should Be Allowed to Occupy Vacant Buildings

Eric Hirsch and Peter Wood

Some homeless people protest city housing policies by squatting. They move into and inhabit abandoned houses, even though such action is illegal. In the following viewpoint, Eric Hirsch and Peter Wood support squatting. They argue that many cities have begun redeveloping run-down neighborhoods by building expensive condominiums and trendy shops, thus displacing the poor people who lived in these neighborhoods. Abandoned houses become the only possible sources of shelter for the homeless, according to the authors. Hirsch is assistant professor of sociology at Columbia University in New York City. Wood is the executive director of the Mutual Housing Association of New York, an organization of squatters who are working to purchase abandoned buildings from the city.

As you read, consider the following questions:

1. What happens to a building when it stands vacant, in the authors' opinion?
2. Why do Hirsch and Wood believe squatting is preferable to other forms of housing development?
3. What is the difference between homesteading and squatting, according to the authors?

Eric Hirsch and Peter Wood, "Squatting in New York City: Justification and Strategy," *Review of Law and Social Change*, vol. XVI, no. 4, 1987-1988. Reprinted with permission of *Review of Law and Social Change*.

As New York City's low-income housing crisis deepens, the unauthorized, illegal occupation of a residence—squatting—becomes an increasingly popular strategy in the city's residential neighborhoods. This is because in New York and in other American cities, market processes and public policies have created a large pool of both underhoused people and abandoned, underutilized housing. The result is a serious, visible problem co-existing with an obvious, visible solution. Since adequate shelter is a matter of survival, those without it are likely to utilize empty buildings even if they do not own those buildings or have the legal right to tenancy. . . .

This article describes an organized squatting campaign which the Association of Community Organizations for Reform Now (ACORN) initiated in 1985 in the East New York neighborhood of Brooklyn. This illegal squatting effort eventually led to a legal homesteading program developed by a new organization, the Mutual Housing Association of New York (MHANY). The East New York example indicates that effective squatting efforts require: local community support for the squatters, effective community organizing to persuade municipal governments to support squatting and rehabilitation in lieu of private sector remedies, financing for adequate rehabilitation of new residences, and careful selection of the squatters to ensure their continuing commitment to the housing program. To explain why this and other squatting efforts are both increasingly common and justified, we must first consider what caused a housing crisis so severe that resort to the controversial act of squatting became inevitable.

Roots of the Problem

Tens of thousands of low-income City residents are homeless. Many can find housing only at rents that place an impossible financial burden on them; others are forced to accept run-down, unsafe apartments. From one perspective, the City does not have enough adequately maintained low-rent apartments. From another, it has too many poor people. . . .

Ineffective Policies

As a result of the trends in job and housing markets, New York City is in desperate need of a large number of decent, low-income housing units. Michael Stegman, the author of two major reports on housing in New York City, estimates that the City needs to build over one-half million housing units in the next decade to meet the current and predicted housing demand. Given the minimal number of housing units currently being added to the stock by private builders, the needed units will not be built without government intervention.

Unfortunately, effective public policy solutions to these problems have not yet been implemented. The rhetoric of "austerity" politics has been used to rationalize inaction on the federal, state, and local levels. Under Ronald Reagan, the federal government took itself out of the public housing construction business. Local policy-makers in post-fiscal crisis New York City worry about whether welfare payments will prevent recipients from accepting poverty-level jobs or whether newly constructed public housing will attract freeloaders. Human Resources Administration Commissioner William Grinker, responding to a proposal to reserve public housing for homeless families, commented: "We don't want to create a demand for homelessness. If families knew that becoming homeless would get them a Housing Authority apartment in a month, it would be a real problem." Rather than providing permanent housing for the homeless, the City's housing policies subsidize gentrification, permit redlining and abandonment, and provide inadequate shelters, transitional housing, and welfare hotels.

Given the large number of units needed by the City's low-income and homeless residents, all available housing resources should be utilized to the utmost. The City-owned *in rem*, or tax-foreclosed, buildings are particularly valuable resources because there are many housing units in the *in rem* buildings and because the rehabilitation of old housing stock is generally cheaper than new construction. If the buildings are allowed to stand vacant, however, they will suffer vandalism and physical deterioration from the elements, making them too costly to rehabilitate. . . .

Encouraging Squatters

The plight of the homeless in our cities is truly deplorable, so are reports of families of six and seven persons living in a single room in a welfare hotel. People who are willing to assume the responsibility of salvaging old apartment buildings should be encouraged by the local governments involved.

Barbara Barna, quoted in *National Review*, March 13, 1987. © 1987 by *National Review*, Inc., 150 East 35 Street, New York, NY 10016. Reprinted with permission.

Given the trends in the private housing market and the inadequate policy response by City officials, the low-income housing crisis may get much worse in the 1990s. Residents of low-income neighborhoods around the city should be aware of a range of strategies which might be used to create additions to their low-income housing stock. One option which has been successfully employed in the East New York neighborhood of Brooklyn is squatting.

East New York has been hurt more than most areas of the City by economic and political trends. Jobs are scarce, and the people who live there are almost entirely minority and poor. Housing problems are severe. City housing policy has not helped. Only about one thousand publicly assisted housing units were added to the neighborhood's stock between 1980 and 1983. Most of the neighborhood's families could not afford these new units, and the construction process contributed to the housing problem by displacing residents and stores.

Like many other poor communities in the City, however, East New York has plenty of potential housing resources in the form of vacant, *in rem* buildings. Until recently, the City's Department of Housing Preservation and Development continued to sponsor auctions of these buildings. This policy turned over most buildings to speculators, who either held the building indefinitely while waiting for its profitable development or again reneged on property taxes. When neighborhood residents did manage to buy a building, they often spent all of their meager resources on its acquisition and thus lacked the financial resources to finance rehabilitation and maintenance costs.

Neighborhood Groups

Neighborhood residents and organizers for a Brooklyn branch of ACORN organized in 1982 to confront the area's serious housing problems. Housing issues were a natural organizing focus because of the obvious, visible nature of both the problem and the solution. Residents of East New York knew the problems: they were themselves homeless or could see the homeless in the streets; they were often doubled up with family or friends in apartments meant for one family; they often spent too much of their income on rent; and they frequently lived in dilapidated units.

The initial organizing effort focused not on homelessness but on abandonment and the fact that abandoned buildings increased the crime rate and reduced property values in ACORN group neighborhoods. These neighborhood groups were later to be vital as political support systems for the squatters. Squatting without such support can involve the undesirable prospect of fighting both the City and one's neighbors. That is not a winning strategy.

At first, the ACORN groups tried to get the City to agree to stop its auctions and to start a homesteading program that would utilize City-owned housing units. The City refused both requests. A series of protests beginning in October 1982 was successful in stopping housing auctions in East New York. But getting a genuine commitment to the homesteading program was more difficult. After a sit-in in the Brooklyn Borough President's office in the spring of 1983, the Borough President agreed to support a pilot, low-income homesteading program, and the City's Department of Housing Preservation and Development (HPD) apparently agreed to fund it. By that winter, however, the program still had not received any funds. After ACORN set up a tent city outside Gracie Mansion, a twenty-eight building housing lottery was held in August 1984, with Mayor Koch making the selections. But another year passed before a single deed was transferred to a homeowner.

Recruitment

By 1985, after three years of frustration, ACORN community groups began to discuss the possibility of squatting in City-owned buildings. There were months of discussions. Staff organizers report that the primary obstacle to gaining a commitment to such a campaign by ACORN's group members was the possibility of the arrest of squatters. Once the strategy was finally approved, the group still had to recruit squatters since most of the ACORN neighborhood group members already had homes or apartments in the neighborhood.

Controversial Strategy

Despite its advantages, squatting can be controversial even among community organizers. . . .

But the low-income housing crisis in the City is so severe that even strategies as controversial as squatting must be seriously considered if they can add a significant number of low-income units to the City's housing stock.

Eric Hirsch and Peter Wood, *New York University Review of Law & Social Change*, vol. XVI, no. 4, 1987/1988.

ACORN tried a number of recruitment strategies. A flyer with ACORN's phone number was distributed. It read simply, "NEED A HOME? DO YOU WANT TO FIGHT THE CITY FOR A HOUSING PROGRAM? CALL ACORN!," and was distributed in the Brooklyn neighborhoods of East New York, Bushwick, Brownsville, Bedford-Stuyvesant, and Crown Heights. Local churches, politicians, social service offices, and Legal Aid and Legal Services offices that deal with housing cases in Brooklyn were all invited to refer potential squatters. Community meetings were held and newspaper advertisements were placed to inform community residents of the squatting effort.

This effort resulted in the recruitment of dozens of families with serious housing needs such as being doubled up with friends or relatives after a recent eviction. Many were Hispanic families who had previously found it difficult to find adequate housing for their large extended families.

Unlike many other housing development plans, this program used only vacant buildings. It did not add to the housing crisis by displacing low-income tenants or homeowners. The squatters themselves often selected the empty buildings used in the campaign. Only City-owned buildings were chosen. Fighting private owners for buildings would have been more difficult to justify to potential squatters and supporters and would have been less likely to succeed. Unlike private owners, the City government is vulnerable to political pressure and was viewed as having a responsibility to house City residents with serious housing needs. . . .

The Settlement

ACORN's successful organizing forced HPD into meaningful negotiations. Perhaps to avoid legitimizing illegal squatting throughout the City, top HPD administrators refused to negotiate directly with ACORN. Instead, the squatters and ACORN activists, in collaboration with the Consumer-Farmer Foundation and the Pratt Institute Center for Community and Environmental Development, created the Mutual Housing Association of New York (MHANY). From this point on, HPD negotiated with this homesteading organization rather than with the squatters or with ACORN. The main advantage of homesteading as opposed to squatting is that homesteading is legal. The program's legal status facilitates fund-raising for the extensive rehabilitation of housing units. Such rehabilitation is crucial. Without it, squatted units remain as only temporary, and often unsafe, housing resources.

The negotiations between the City and MHANY resulted in a settlement in the fall of 1987 when the City agreed to turn over the deeds to fifty-eight buildings with 180 units of housing, to commit nearly $3 million to rehabilitate the buildings (since increased to $11 million), and to cooperate closely with the former squatters in the creation of scores of new units of housing for the low-income residents of East New York.

MHANY rigorously screened potential recruits for the homesteading program. The procedure identified those recruits with the greatest need for housing. Each potential family had to show that its total income was less than eighty percent of the standard metropolitan statistical area median. The seriousness of a family's housing problems—such as overcrowding, high rent-to-income ratios, recent eviction or displacement—was also considered in the process. No one who owned property in the New York City area or had lost property because of nonpayment of property taxes was allowed into the program. An attempt was also made to match building or unit size with the housing needs of the homesteading family.

A program which recruited solely on the basis of housing needs, however, could fail because of the inability of some homesteaders to accomplish the daunting physical and financial task of rehabilitating run-down buildings. To demonstrate their commitment, each family had to put in a minimum of fifty hours of supervised sweat-equity work on their building before they would be considered for the program. Each family, moreover, not only had to submit a statement of understanding detailing their interest and goals in joining the homesteading effort, but was also expected to attend meetings and to complete three workshops on how the program would operate. All families had to prove their financial capability to undertake the future maintenance of their building.

Militant Squatters

The passion of the more militant squatters is fueled by the sense that the city and federal governments are waging a war against the poor. "Housing is a military issue," says Kenny Tolias, a five-year veteran of the squatting wars. "It's about forcing people out of the inner cities." For Tolias and the other hardliners, New York City's high-powered maneuvers around the squats and in the park constitute further proof of "Spatial Deconcentration," a concerted plan by federal bureaucrats to clear out the poor and potentially riotous minorities in order to pave the way for neighborhood "revitalization." Squatters view themselves as the last stand against gentrification, which helps explain their willingness to hurl themselves against police barricades.

Sarah Ferguson, *The Village Voice*, July 18, 1989.

To ensure that the rehabilitated units remained in the low-income housing stock for the foreseeable future, MHANY places limits on the resale value of the rehabilitated homesteading units. MHANY splits the deed to each mortgage, separating the land from the building. The building deed goes to the homesteader or to a housing cooperative while the land is placed in a ninety-nine year trust. The land trust deed takes these units out of the private housing market by stipulating restrictions on the resale of the property. Homesteaders can remain in their unit as long as they wish and can pass their unit on to members of their immediate family. But if a family decides to move, MHANY can buy the unit for resale to another low-income family on its waiting list, or it can restrict the sale price of the building to what the previous owner paid. In this manner, the land trust allows the community to slow gentrification, to put rental units under internally mandated rent control, to provide a vehicle for the program's enforcement, and to conserve capital for future maintenance needs.

MHANY also is designed to solve one of the most difficult problems with sweat-equity models of development—the lack of financial resources for rehabilitation and for continued maintenance of the housing units. It has received low-interest loans from area banks and has convinced the City to sell its buildings to the homesteaders for one dollar per building and to make a forgivable loan of $2.7 million for the rehabilitation of the homes. The City has also agreed to a twenty-year tax abatement program and has set aside $2 million in rehabilitation money from the Federal Department of Housing and Urban Development for the homesteading effort. The Consumer-Farmer Foundation has helped with financing administrative and planning costs. The Pratt Center—under a technical services contract with the City—has developed plans for the rehabilitation of the housing units under the provisions of the City's building code. The City has accepted a two-year schedule for installation of major systems in the buildings and has allowed five years to obtain certificates of occupancy.

MHANY has thus created a social contract between itself, homesteaders, and the City. Homesteaders provide physical labor for rehabilitation, get cheap housing, and agree not to profit from the resale of their building. The city provides the *in rem* units and funds for their rehabilitation and gets a large stock of low-income housing. MHANY provides for administrative coordination of the effort and raises additional rehabilitation funds. The model represents one of the most effective solutions to the low-income housing crisis devised to date.

A Justified Approach

The extent of the low-income housing crisis indicates that the current system of delivering housing resources does not adequately meet the needs of many New York City residents. Putting the provision of housing primarily in the private sector has meant that many lower-income residents of New York City will not be provided with housing. Uneven economic development, and austerity policies that reinforce such development, have created widespread poverty, homelessness, doubling up, over-crowding, high rent-to-income ratios, poor housing quality, and a large stock of abandoned, City-owned buildings. Both the most severe housing problems and the bulk of the publicly owned buildings are located in the City's poorest neighborhoods.

Under such crisis conditions, a variety of strategies—including illegal ones—must be utilized to add units to the City's low-income housing stock. ACORN activists originally attempted to gain support for their homesteading program through legal means. It was only the endless foot-dragging by a City administration committed to ineffective private sector policies that necessitated the illegal squatting approach. The severity of the housing crisis meant that residents had to use extraordinary means to force the City to respond to the urgent needs of East New York residents.

The squatting effort and the homesteading program which followed is accomplishing much. One hundred and eighty units of permanent, rehabilitated, low-income housing are being created because ACORN and their supporters decided to squat in those East New York buildings. The organizing model used by the group ensured that the squatters' neighbors would support the effort and that the squatters would have the resources and ability to rehabilitate their buildings successfully. Criteria established by a community-controlled board guarantee that only those with serious housing needs and the ability to carry out a successful homesteading effort will be approved as homesteaders. Recruiting potential homesteaders from the City's waiting lists for public and City-owned housing would not accomplish this goal.

ACORN has demonstrated how effective community organizing can pressure the City to release its low-income housing stock to poor City residents. MHANY has shown one way to maintain affordable housing for low-income families. Of course, this model would have to be implemented on a much larger scale to make a dent in the serious, Citywide, low-income housing crisis. What is needed is an organized squatting movement by the City's poor and underhoused to convince the City to provide for their housing needs and a housing development model that creates and preserves more low-income units than it destroys. That, along with effective anti-poverty policies and other housing development models—including public housing construction—is required if the City is to meet the housing needs of its poor residents.

"It would be wrong to say that squatting is a way out of the city's absurd and vicious housing policy."

The Homeless Should Not Be Allowed to Occupy Vacant Buildings

Peter Weber

Peter Weber is a free-lance writer living in New York. In the following viewpoint, he describes his trip to New York's Lower East Side, where most of the illegal occupation of abandoned buildings, known as squatting, occurs. Weber contends that most squatters are young white radicals. The squatting movement, he argues, is not helping truly needy homeless people.

As you read, consider the following questions:

1. What beliefs motivate young people to occupy abandoned houses, according to Weber?
2. Why does the author believe many buildings are abandoned?
3. How does Weber argue that squatting hurts innocent landlords?

Peter Weber, "Scenes from the Squatting Life," *National Review*, February 27, 1987. © 1987 by *National Review, Inc.*, 150 East 35 Street, New York, NY 10016, Reprinted with permission.

"As you can see, it needs a little work." Yes, we could see that. For one thing, there was no staircase (it was a seven-story building), and we peered from the first floor landing up to the sky, through six stories of filth and old beams and swathes of rotted metal that seemed to hang precariously above our heads. It was not dark, because there were huge sections of wall missing, through which we could see the abandoned building next door. To get from the first floor to the second you climb a long, thin ladder from a fire escape that has been propped up against the second-floor landing under all those suspended palm leaves of metal. To get to the upper floors you go to the back and climb (prayerfully) up the tilting fire escape itself. Amidst all the rubble and dirt and holes in the floors were several "apartments" people had cleared out for themselves. . . .

The Lower East Side

I had come to New York's Lower East Side because everybody had said, for squatting, that's the place. Like many areas of New York City, the Lower East Side has whole blocks of abandoned buildings now owned by the city and left to deteriorate. Everywhere you see signs claiming the buildings for some local activist group or other. That doesn't mean they own them: They are claiming them on various principles. It wasn't hard to guess at one possible principle. In a city in which rights to a rent-controlled apartment can start a blood feud, the city government has acquired, primarily through tax defaults, roughly ten thousand residential buildings, accounting for more than 120,000 units of housing; 5,717 of these buildings (more than seventy thousand units) are vacant. Another 118,000 units are currently in default and could be taken over at any time. . . .

Squatting has begun to catch on in the United States. Here as in Europe it has gained a foothold mostly in cities with tightly regulated housing markets, such as New York City and Washington, D.C. In Amsterdam the city owns 75 per cent of the land; in Harlem the city owns 70 per cent of the buildings. There are squatters' organizations in the United States, some clearly inspired by their European cousins, talking homes for the poor out of one side of their mouths and the destruction of capitalism out of the other. So I went down to the Lower East Side to find out whether New York's squatters were just punked-out drug dealers, agents of Godless Communism, or the truly needy. Also, I've been looking for a two-bedroom condo, with eat-in kitchen and lots of light, for months.

After poking around the neighborhood, I walked over to the local soup kitchen, and some friendly people there offered to introduce me to some squatters. . . .

Some squatters tend toward ideology or inverted class snobbery, but these kids were real egalitarians: "We accept both punk rockers and skinheads. We don't discriminate." "My parents are *yuppies*," said one unfortunate, a black kid from Chicago, looking sheepish; "they got money." One chunky guy from Westchester ("I hate to commute") told us about the squatters next door, whose place had become quite sophisticated and comfortable. Who lived there? Well, at one time or another he had seen at least three of the oppressed coming out of there in business suits.

Subsidizing Squatting

Elzie Robinson is an 85-year-old former janitor who owns four buildings in Harlem. A big, robust man, painfully slowed by age, he still spends all day every day tending his eighty-four apartments.

On March 3, 1986, New York City Housing Court Judge Lewis Friedman threw him in jail for not providing adequate heat and hot water for people in his buildings. The "tenants" were actually squatters who moved into one of his buildings after it was damaged by fire. Judge Friedman told Robinson, who is black, that it made no difference—as long as people were in his building he was obligated to provide them with services.

William Tucker, *The American Spectator*, July 1986.

Later we hung out in front of another building (no reporters allowed inside) and eyeballed some of the graffiti: "No entry for gentry." "Kill gentry." "The rich get richer and the poor get evicted." We watched some of the squatters come and go—it was a bustling little building. For the most part, they were kids, college-age, white, articulate, pausing to speak on the housing problem or the homeless, but then rushing off to lectures at NYU or to eat the food churches give out for the truly poor. One of them, a young woman, was dressed in leather and sported an attractive plastic spider in her ear. Four years' college, year in Italy, corporate job, which she quit, hadn't had a shower in nine days. She moved to this building because there was a heavy drug scene in the homestead across the street. She said she hardly ever talks to her parents, except for the time her mother saw her on TV brushing her teeth at a fire hydrant and sent her father out looking for her in the richmobile. She does what other kids around do. Work, maybe. Maybe hand out passes for the Aztec, the Pyramid, or Danceteria. Get drunk, do drugs.

In Search of Authentic Squatters

Meanwhile, through the grapevine, we began to hear of a more "authentic" squatting operation, with real neighborhood people and a good reputation, and we thought we'd better check it out.

Dumi (not his real name) is a large, articulate, and very likable black photographer. He has a full beard, wears baggy green pants, and gives the impression he's always rolling around at you. He loves to talk, which he says is "the artist flow in me," and is a shaker and mover in a successful squatting operation. Their buildings were in relatively good shape to begin with, but Dumi and his fellow squatters have fixed them up, and have seventy or so tenants. The hitch is that they never paid anything for the buildings, and technically the city still owns them.

Now Dumi was going to meet some new serious squatters a few blocks north. On the way over he talked energetically—you have to like this guy—about the Cause, about "taking it to the UN," about how "we're talking World Court level. . . . We want the world to know about the atrocities going on here." And now, finally, I was going over to meet some of the really oppressed, the truly needy, the salt of the city, who had to squat to survive and were also standing up for their rights.

Makeshift Radicals

Well, this scene became clear right away on the front steps. Two of the squatters were young white guys, fashionably dressed; the third was a pleasant-looking if plump white lady, in her forties perhaps, wearing baggy but clean clothes, complicated brass filigree earrings, and a Mao cap with a red star on the front. We got a tour of the mess they were calling home, and Dumi was excited because the staircase was intact. Otherwise, it was pure filth.

In a dingy front room was a kind of office with a telephone, which appeared to be the headquarters of a makeshift radical organization with a service called Eviction Watch and an "emergency" number. One of the well-dressed white guys had been sitting by the phone for days at a time, but nobody ever called. There were posters up about La Huelga and genocide, literature on "the war against the poor," and copies of *Our Land: The Magazine for Those Who Refuse to Move*, which offered suggestions on stealing food from local merchants.

The Need for Grass-Roots

The three squatters wanted to know how they could get some real black and Hispanic people interested in their project. They had tried: They had handed out applications at a local church, made speeches and had them translated into Spanish: but no takers. That was bad—they needed to become more grass-roots. They also wanted to know how they could steal electric power from Con Ed. Dumi . . . gave them a bunch of advice. He liked them, he liked the fact that their building had a staircase, he saw possibilities for some kind of organization here. He told them that once they got a few families with kids they could go to Con Ed and tell them they had kids living in here and they didn't want to steal and would pay. Then, having legitimate electricity and getting mail and having a telephone—and of course having kids in the building—would give them more leverage when they had to pressure the authorities. Well, Dumi was ready for meetings. "If you guys think we could get together on a serious plane, I'm down." He wanted them to meet Manuel, who had done so much for his own homestead.

Squatting Isn't the Answer

The city's housing policy, by its arbitrariness, lacks the character of law and has thus steadily eroded property rights in housing.

Squatting isn't the answer to the city's housing policy.

On the way over I asked the guy I had shrewdly pegged as the real revolutionary (intense stare, wire-rim glasses) how he had gotten involved: "I needed an apartment." I asked him about gentrification. More candor: He understood a lot of neighborhood people were for it and that was understandable, since it had probably been responsible for Operation Pressure Point (a police project for cleaning up the drug traffic) and had improved the area and had created jobs—even if those jobs meant working for the gentry—"although *I* couldn't work for them," he said.

Meeting Manuel

The little band marched over to meet Manuel, who was working with fellow tenants to replace sewage pipes in the basement. The first thing he did when he saw these three intense white people with the Mao cap and the wire-rim glasses was to ask how many Hispanic, black, and neighborhood people they had for their building. "Well," they said, "that's something we wanted to ask you about. . . ." Manuel was getting the idea right away. They had a fragmented conversation, and when somebody actually mentioned the word "revolution" Manuel said, "What revolution? We're trying to fix up a building!" Manuel is from the South Bronx and has seen people freeze to death. He wants a building with neighborhood people, families, people in need—but almost all he can come up with (as I began to find out here too) is educated white and artist types. He was not thrilled to take on these radical petty-criminal characters with secret agendas. . . .

Dumi wanted to arrange a "meet," but Manuel just said, "Sorry, not interested," producing 1.75 seconds of astounded silence. The candid revolutionary, who was a pretty subtle guy, ideologically speaking, was saying they had to have such people, "Otherwise we're just low-rent gentrifiers." I thought maybe he'd hit on something there.

All these buildings I visited downtown were city-owned. Manuel and almost everyone else I spoke with responded in exactly the same way when I asked if they would squat in an abandoned but privately owned building: "Oh no," they told me, "that would be trespassing." Another ideological subtlety, but it turns out that the subtleties of ideology are the life-blood of the New York squatting scene. . . .

ACORN

Meanwhile, over in Brooklyn, pandemonium. The meeting has almost begun, but for the past 15 minutes Mr. Camacho and Mr. Colon have been yelling at each other at the top of their lungs. Mr. Camacho is very mad: He was away in Puerto Rico for six months, came back, and still doesn't have a house. He's still on the waiting list. They yell back and forth until the meeting starts, and then for some time afterward. Finally order is restored, and business can get under way in the basement of ACORN's offices on Flatbush Avenue. ACORN stands for the Association of Community Organizations for Reform Now; it's a national organization involved in different kinds of agitation and causes, from rent strikes to pressuring banks to reduce fees for bounced checks. If those at the meeting are any indication, ACORN's New York staff consists mostly of young white radicals who don't believe in property, while its membership consists mostly of older Hispanic folks who would like to acquire some. They are there because ACORN says it can get them houses for free, if they are willing to fix them up.

Through its brand of civil disobedience, which in this case consists of its members squatting and getting arrested, ACORN is trying to get the city to give over some 33 houses and the land under them without charge—in fact, with accompanying loans. Along with this outflow of government money, it is also seeking what your realtor might call creative financing. ACORN has been demonstrating in front of Banco de Ponce for a loan, hoping the bank will give in to political pressure and cough up a three-year $100,000 loan interest free. (ACORN is known for such tactics as busing in several hundred people to occupy a single bank office.)

Not the Truly Needy

I went out to bleak East New York one Saturday morning where some ACORN members were having a work party to get running water for one of their squatters. They had gotten a permit to dig a hole in the pavement in order to turn on the water valve, and now they were duly filling up the hole with blacktop, using a jackhammer on loan from the employer of one of the members. The only illegality they commit, they said, is the squatting itself.

Inside the two-family house—which was in sad shape overall, having sat unoccupied except by drug dealers for years—I met the squatters, a charming young woman named Luisa, her husband, and their three children. She said they had been in the building for about a year, and their own area seemed reasonably livable. I asked if Luisa worked, and she told me she was a doctor. A medical doctor? Yes, she had just finished her internship in the Dominican Republic and was waiting to take the boards here in the United States. Her husband worked in a video store owned by his mother. He took home, Luisa said, about $350 a week.

Not the truly needy; but not vandals or anarchists either. Indeed, except for those thousands of city-owned abandoned buildings, and ACORN's political skills, the idea of squatting would certainly never have occurred to these people. However Luisa and her husband justify breaking the law, and whatever the vagaries of Manuel's ideology, it was clear that what all these people really wanted was to become homeowners, not the beneficiaries of a socialist state. As Professor Peter Salins commented, "Once squatters get control they behave like landlords." I remembered Dumi had told me how he and his fellow squatters had refused to move from their apartments, citing laws about illegal eviction; but later they bodily evicted a tenant they suspected of drug dealing, without anything resembling due process. (Good thing, too: In his apartment they found drug paraphernalia, a bullet-proof vest, and spent shells.)

But it would be wrong to say that squatting is a way out of the city's absurd and vicious housing policy. Manuel and Dumi and Luisa don't prove anything except that even in a state of nature the good guys sometimes win. The city's housing policy, by its arbitrariness, lacks the character of law and has thus steadily eroded property rights in housing. Squatting isn't the answer to the city's housing policy, it *is* the city's housing policy, for when the rule of law is abolished in favor of the war of all against all, possession is a good deal more than nine-tenths of the law.

The Darker Side

The dark side of squatting is best illustrated by a story I pursued only after reading about it in a remarkable article on rent control in *The American Spectator* by William Tucker. Tucker had written about Mr. Elzie Robinson, an 85-year-old Harlem landlord who had squatters of his own, local citizens not quite up to the fine distinctions between city and private buildings that seemed so clear to Manuel and his friends. I went uptown to pay him a visit, and found him sunning himself in front of his office. He offered to show me the building where he was having all the problems.

He owns several buildings on the block—decent, well-maintained buildings with steady tenants. But this one had had a fire. He wanted to fix the place up, but from the beginning people had moved into it from the street. Then one of the squatters—who according to Mr. Robinson had never paid a cent of rent money—had him taken to court to restore the services lost since the fire. She won. The 85-year-old Mr. Robinson was thrown in jail by Judge Friedman of New York's Housing Court, and ordered to maintain basic services for the squatters—heat, electricity, plumbing. No matter that they had come in uninvited and had never paid rent and clearly never would. No matter that if Mr. Robinson bricks up the apartments, the next day someone has clawed his way in. Once he actually succeeded in having a man evicted, only to go back and find that the man's daughter had moved in—and Mr. Robinson had to start up the whole process again. (It can take more than six months to get someone evicted.) . . .

This is the other side of squatting. With respect to abandoned buildings you could call it part of the city's supply side: Soon these people would drive Mr. Robinson's building into bankruptcy. Then the city could take over the building and, unless the city itself were unusually diligent, the squatters could go on living there unperturbed by whatever minute pangs of conscience they might feel now.

A Squatter and a Junkie

Back outside we sat on a bench, and Mr. Robinson pointed out some of his "tenants," sitting on the hood of a car, doing drug transactions in broad daylight. Down the block cars rolled up, rolled away. I talked to a nervous-looking man Mr. Robinson had identified as a squatter and a junkie, who had been hanging out near one of the car windows. He was young to middle-aged, bearded, wore an old green jacket, and seemed to be sweating lightly. He told me he had been in the building since 1979. How much rent did he pay? I asked. End of smile. End of eye contact. He started staring at a point in the distance and commenced a remarkable process of hemming and hawing—"Well, hmm, hah, hmmm . . ."—and he actually came up with a figure: $105. When was the last time he paid? "Ah! Hah, hmmm . . ." and then he said, "Why . . . just last month . . . or so . . . hmmm." Mr. Robinson was grinning from ear to ear. "Steve," he said, "how can you stand there and say that? You know you ain't paid me a cent since you been here." "Hmm, well, hmm. . . ." Then Steve's face flashed suddenly from humble compliance and confusion into that strange mixture of hatred, anger, guilt, indignation—and he pointed at Mr. Robinson, saying, "See *you* later, Boss." And he stalked away, perhaps thinking how at least that judge downtown would be on his side.

"We call for a reinvigorated public housing program as the basis of a new federal commitment to housing the very poor."

More Public Housing Would Help the Homeless

David C. Schwartz, Richard C. Ferlauto, and Daniel N. Hoffman

In the following viewpoint, David C. Schwartz, Richard C. Ferlauto, and Daniel N. Hoffman argue that the first step in reducing homelessness should be building more public housing. The number of people needing low-income housing will increase, they predict, making more affordable housing essential. Schwartz is a political science professor at Rutgers University in New Brunswick, New Jersey. He is chairman of the board of the National Housing Institute, a New Jersey-based organization which trains tenants groups. Ferlauto is a community organizer and legislative analyst to numerous community-based organizations. Hoffman is a consultant on housing and urban economic development.

As you read, consider the following questions:

1. Who benefits from supplemental income programs such as vouchers, according to the authors?
2. Why do Schwartz, Ferlauto, and Hoffman object to privately owned low-income housing?
3. Why is public housing a good investment, in the authors' opinion?

David C. Schwartz, Richard C. Ferlauto, and Daniel N. Hoffman, eds. *A New Housing Policy for America*. Philadelphia: Temple University Press, 1988. Reprinted with permission.

The 1980s witnessed a scandalous explosion in homelessness. Federal cutbacks in housing supply and rental assistance for the poor tended to increase this tragic phenomenon. Surely Ronald Reagan's announced view that most homeless people are on the streets by choice bespoke not even the kind of recognition of the facts from which decent policy might flow. National housing policy in the 1980s, a policy of knowing neglect of our public housing inventory and manifest unconcern about the stagnation and decline in the quality of our housing stock, is more apt to produce homelessness than homeownership.

In the 1990s America will require more housing, better targeted to the life needs of an increasingly diverse population. . . .

Public Housing

For millions of Americans the dream of homeownership is not practicable. For some, high costs make homeownership unaffordable, while for others, life circumstances make property ownership undesirable. For tens of millions of poor Americans, and for many elderly, single, and handicapped persons, the dream is simply to have decent, safe, affordable rental housing. It is incumbent upon us to offer a program that addresses this dream too.

It was the need to develop decent, safe, affordable housing, and equally importantly to create construction jobs during the Great Depression, that first involved the federal government in public housing programs and policy. Public housing did not start out as housing for the very poor. Senator Robert Wagner of New York, principal author of the Housing Act of 1937 said, "There are some who we cannot expect to serve, . . . those who cannot pay the rent." In the fifty years since the passage of the first housing act, the role of public housing has changed. Public housing is now the housing provider of last resort for those who would otherwise have no shelter.

The public housing tenant of the 1980s is very poor and getting poorer relative to the rest of society. Ten percent of all the nation's renters whose incomes are less than 50 percent of their area's median live in public housing. A 1981 HUD [Housing and Urban Development] survey indicates that 65 percent of all public housing incomes are between 10 percent and 30 percent of the area median, 89 percent between 10 percent and 50 percent of the area median. Incomes of families living in public housing average about $6,000 per year; elderly tenants (38 percent of all public housing tenants) have even lower annual incomes, averaging about $5,000, with 70 percent having incomes between $3,000 and $6,000 per year. The overall average income of renters in public housing in 1983 was $5,360, or 24 percent of the national median.

As noted earlier, the federal government has supported public housing construction programs since 1937. It has also experimented with a variety of other deep-subsidy housing construction programs during the past 20 years. Some of these programs, such as Section 236, Section 8 New Construction, and the original Public Housing Program, have sought to increase the supply of standard, low-rent housing. Other programs, such as rent vouchers, Section 23, and the Section 8 Existing Certificate Program, have sought to supplement the incomes of poor tenants so that they could afford market-rate rents. In total, more than 4 million households have been assisted by federal housing activities. As we look toward a new housing policy, we need to examine both supplemental income and supply programs.

Solving the Problem

How much will it cost to solve the housing mess? . . .

Public subsidies are too costly, too inefficient, and ultimately too ineffective. The solution lies with federally funded, nonprofit housing of various forms.

Richard P. Appelbaum, *Society*, May/June 1989.

The theory behind supplemental income rental programs is that even low-income housing consumers should have some choice regarding where they want to live, as long as the unit is not substandard and is rented at a reasonable rate. The theory also holds that, in response to the greater purchasing power of low-income renters, the market will build new standard housing at prices that the rental certificate or voucher holders could afford. However, despite extensive studies there is little evidence to suggest that supplemental income programs have spurred the construction or alleviated shortages of low-cost rental housing. A 1982 HUD report found that more than half of white recipients and nearly three-quarters of minority recipients who received Section 8 Certificates failed to find units. Many local housing authorities report higher failure rates, due to lack of available units. Because these programs have not encouraged additional supply, no residual number of vacated units for other low-income renters has resulted. There has been no benefit from these programs for low-income renters as a class. Only those who directly receive benefits (as tenants or landlords) are helped by supplemental income housing assistance. Furthermore, even that advantage is short-term. These programs provide assistance for a specified period, during which time substantial public expenditures are made. At the end of the period, assistance may be terminated despite a continuing need. The end result is that a poor family is again without decent, safe, and affordable housing, and a substantial sum of public money is gone. Because these programs do not provide a permanent source of affordable housing either for the program participant or for the taxpayer, whose money has been spent for a fleeting benefit, we believe that supplemental income housing assistance programs are not a worthwhile strategy. We would urge the phasing out of this type of program.

Privately Owned Housing

The federal government also has extensive experience with construction programs that do increase the supply of affordable housing. Unlike the certificate or voucher programs, construction programs increase housing availability for those directly housed in a development, as well as for those who are able to occupy units vacated (which may or may not be affordable for low-income tenants). Originally, the principal construction program was public housing, housing owned and operated by public entities. However, in an effort to involve the private sector and reduce the costs of what was perceived to be an expensive program, the federal government established the Section 221(d)(3) Below Market Interest Rate (BMIR), Section 236, Section 8, and Section 515 programs. Under each of these programs, private entities were responsible for owning and operating low-income housing. More than 1.9 million units were produced and made available to low-income renters by these programs.

In return for private participation, the programs were structured to allow private owners to leave the various programs at the end of a 15- or 20-year period, depending on the program. These programs have been providing affordable opportunities during the past 15 and 20 years. But property owners are now choosing to leave these programs in order to take advantage of changed real estate conditions. Thousands of residents have been forced to move and recent analyses by the Congressional Budget Office and the General Accounting Office indicate that hundreds of thousands of units are "at risk" of being lost due to prepayment of mortgages. By 1995, 900,000 tenant households may be threatened with displacement or substantially increased rents. By the year 2025 the at-risk population will include nearly all households living in the 1.9 million Section 221 (d)(3) BMIR, 8,236, and 515 units. . . .

Our national housing policy has been shortsighted. Participation by the private sector in the 236, 221(d)(3), and Section 8 New Construction programs was supposed to save the taxpayers money over what would have been spent if the units had been developed as public housing. In fact, the Section 8 New Construction Program's per-unit subsidy is four times greater than the public housing subsidy. Section 236 units may require only about half the subsidy of public housing units, but if they are lost from the nation's low-rent housing stock after 15 or 20 years they will not have been less expensive. Furthermore, Section 236 tenants in 1983 had an average annual income of 43 percent of the national median in-

come, an amount 75 percent greater than that of the typical public housing tenant and high enough to allow them to obtain affordable shelter in a shallow-subsidy state program.

And public housing is an appreciating national asset. Public housing today has a replacement value of more than $70 billion. It is tragic for the families affected that we are faced with the problem of units reverting to the open market. It is also a scandal that the spending of tax dollars will have resulted in market-rate rental units and condominiums rather than the shelter for the poor that the taxpayers had a right to expect.

Lessons from the Past

The past 20 years of federal housing policy have taught us several lessons. We now know that supplemental income rental assistance programs do not alleviate low-rent housing shortages. We now know that programs that do not permanently add to the low-rent housing stock will create needlessly uncertain futures for poor tenants. We now know that programs that do not permanently add to the low-rent housing stock are more expensive to develop and operate than public housing, particularly considering that these units can disappear from the low-rent housing stock after 15 or 20 years of receiving extensive public subsidies. Finally, we now know that we will need deeply subsidized low-income housing for the foreseeable future.

Based upon 1974-1983 trends, it is projected that by 1993 there will be 7.5 million unsubsidized low-rent units available, but there will be more than 14.3 million families in need of such units. More than 17 million families will need low-rent units by 2003, but only about 7 million units will be in the marketplace. We need a federal housing policy that builds new publicly owned units that will be a permanent part of the nation's low-rent housing stock. Fortunately, we have the makings of such a program; it is public housing. More than 1.3 million families in nearly 3,200 communities call public housing home. . . .

A New Commitment

We call for a reinvigorated public housing program as the basis of a new federal commitment to housing the very poor. The federal government should produce 40,000 public housing units annually. Compared to zero units or 4,000 units, 40,000 units is a lot of housing. However, it is only 90 percent of the number of public housing units produced in 1979. . . .

Public housing does have a checkered history. Cost containment should be a priority, but it must not come at the expense of proper building design or maintenance. Neither the tenant nor society is advantaged by constructing sparse units that fail to meet the physical, familial, and community needs of tenants. In seeking to build upon public housing's successful experiences, the federal government must develop a system that is sensibly designed and properly maintained. We are all familiar with the high-rise horror stories of Pruitt-Igoe and more recently the demolition of Scudder Homes in Newark. But the fact is that most modern public housing projects, those built during the past 20 years, have averaged well under 100 units in size. HUD should continue to develop modest-sized projects. In addition to modest scale, sensibly designed housing must include modern appliances, landscaping, and recreational and social facilities. Stark housing and the absence of amenities does not encourage communitarian behavior, so vital to the success of public housing. . . .

The federal government must be committed to being a partner and a friend of the poor, for the federal government is the only partner capable of providing the resources that the poor need. Helping the poor become self-sufficient and productive members of society should be a national goal. Decent, safe, affordable shelter is a prerequisite for self-sufficiency. It is counterproductive public policy, and indecent moral policy, to reduce direct housing assistance to the poor. We can and must do better.

"Vouchers are . . . an effective way to reduce the cost of housing to the poor."

Vouchers Would Help the Homeless

Kenneth J. Beirne

One housing policy often suggested to help low-income people, including the homeless, is vouchers. Unlike traditional public housing programs, in which low-income people live in federally built housing projects, with vouchers people may choose where they want to live, and the government pays a significant portion of the rent. In the following viewpoint, Kenneth J. Beirne argues that vouchers are an efficient way to help the homeless, since they use already existing housing. Beirne is a former assistant secretary in the Department of Housing and Urban Development and a public policy expert for The Heritage Foundation, a conservative Washington, D.C. think tank.

As you read, consider the following questions:

1. What are the two main housing problems of the poor, according to the author?
2. Why does Beirne criticize public housing?
3. How does the author answer criticisms of the voucher program?

Kenneth J. Beirne, "Vouchers: A Way to Provide Better Housing for America's Poor," The Heritage Foundation *Backgrounder*, May 27, 1987. Reprinted by permission.

It has become increasingly evident to lawmakers that America's low-income housing programs need a drastic overhaul. Most major cities are blighted by public housing projects that have become neighborhoods of hopelessness and decay. And the cost of public sector-financed housing typically is 40 percent higher than private costs—meaning the same expenditures serve fewer families. . . .

Housing vouchers would provide low-income Americans with the funds to exercise real choice in the rental market. Vouchers also would tackle the two main housing problems of low-income Americans. The first of these is rental costs. Since there now exists an adequate national stock of decent housing, the issue for poor families is affordability, not supply. The second problem is that the poor find it difficult to move to new neighborhoods for better jobs or education when they are effectively confined to public housing and other government-sponsored projects. These supply-based programs prevent families from pursuing the best employment, educational, and social opportunities.

Affording Market Rents

Both problems are alleviated by vouchers, which provide families with the means to pay market rents and place few limits on their movement or place of residence. Moreover, because of the enormous cost of housing families in newly constructed buildings, vouchers enabling the poor to use the existing rental market make it possible to house more than twice as many families for the same outlays. . . .

It is now widely accepted that successful welfare reform hinges on the availability of employment and training for welfare recipients. Employment opportunities depend in large part on the ability of those seeking jobs to relocate near available jobs. U.S. history is a testimony to the extraordinary geographical mobility of the American worker. Yet public housing and other construction programs limit the mobility of the poor and thus their access to employment and training. The use of housing vouchers is the only current housing strategy that can give poor families the flexibility to pursue jobs.

Another advantage of vouchers is their cost effectiveness, compared to alternative housing programs. Construction of housing under federal programs, for example, has been costing 20-40 percent more per unit than privately built and operated units. In all, the taxpayer cost of new housing for a typical low-income family was over $6,000 per year in 1981, more than twice the cost of housing a family with vouchers. On an equivalent basis, housing a family through new construction today would cost over $8,000 per year.

The trouble is that despite this high cost, poor families have not been well served. Those who could obtain federally owned or assisted housing often found themselves in badly located, dismal projects, far away from available jobs and education. Federal and local governments, concerned about the concentration of poor families in the cities, attempted to force low-income housing into middle-class and suburban areas—with no great success and much vocal resistance.

Earlier recognition of these problems had already led to the exploration of alternatives. In 1972, Congress launched the Experimental Housing Allowance Program (EHAP). This demonstration was designed to test all the aspects of a voucher-style program in 16 sites across the nation, from the effects on demand for housing and supply of housing, to the success of families in finding units, using vouchers and the effect of including a "shoppers incentive" by allowing families to keep the money they saved on rent. In fact, EHAP aid proved the potential for success of a nationwide voucher program over seven years of exhaustive data gathering. In 1974, even while the EHAP was being conducted, Congress authorized the Section 8 Existing housing program, which provided rent subsidies for families living in certain existing private rental housing. By 1981 this program was providing housing for less than half the cost of new construction programs.

Empowering the Poor

The problem for the poor is not the unavailability of housing, but a lack of sufficient funds to pay for quality housing. Vouchers give the poor the funds that make this private housing affordable. The demand for quality housing created by vouchers would stimulate construction of private housing where necessary. . . .

Numerous studies and demonstration projects show that vouchers can deliver superior housing assistance to a low-income family at less than half the cost of constructing a new unit with federal support.

Charles L. Heatherly and Burton Yale Pines, *Mandate for Leadership II: Policy Strategies for the 1990s*, 1989.

Building on these experiences and on studies revealing that there is an adequate supply of standard housing, the President's Commission on Housing in 1982 recommended that housing assistance rely primarily on a voucher program.

Since most lawmakers have recognized that new housing construction is much too costly, Congress and the Administration since 1981 have had only two practical choices for providing housing to the poor: vouchers or the Section 8 Existing program. Both address the needs of poor families, those whose household incomes fall below 50 percent of the median in the area in which they live.

The Section 8 program provides certificates to renters that allow the landlord to obtain a subsidy for housing the certificate holder. Both the voucher program and the certificate program supplement the tenant's direct payment of rent, thereby allowing poor families to obtain affordable housing.

How Section 8 Works

A Section 8 family can rent any apartment within the jurisdiction of its Public Housing Authority (PHA) that is available at a rent below what is known as the "Fair Market Rent" (FMR). The FMR is set at the rent paid by at least 45 percent of the families moving within a market area in the most recent two years. This means that poor families theoretically can reside in housing units at least as good as those occupied by 45 percent of the area's inhabitants.

In recent years, the PHA has had the flexibility to write contracts with any landlord the tenant wishes—so long as the unit's rental is below the FMR. In practice, however, tenants and the PHAs deal mainly with already participating Section 8 landlords. One reason for this is that under the Section 8 program landlords must rent their units initially for no more than the FMR. However, rent of each unit is automatically adjusted each year to compensate for inflation—regardless of the state of the rental market, in which rents might even be falling. The federal subsidy to landlords rises according to this rent adjustment. If these adjusted rents rise significantly above the actual market, HUD can require that they be brought back into line with market conditions when the units are vacated or rerented. But in practice there is always a tendency for such action to lag behind rent increases, and further, HUD can be fiercely resisted by well-connected local landlords and politicians. The result is that in most markets the annual adjustment effectively means a guaranteed rent increase and more money from Uncle Sam. Not surprisingly, landlords like Section 8.

A second reason why PHAs stay with existing landlords is that paperwork and inspection requirements are greatly simplified for officials who deal with an established stable of landlords.

How Vouchers Work

A poor family using a housing voucher is not constrained by the Section 8 conditions that prevent a family from paying more than 30 percent of its income for rent. With a voucher, a family could choose to pay more and locate in a suburban section of its PHA's market area, near good schools and employment prospects. The vouchers thus provide valuable economic, educational, and social flexibility. In contrast to a Section 8 certificate, a voucher has universal "portability."

The value of the voucher paid to a family is based on the difference between the Payment Standard (identical to the Section

8 FMR in the first year) and 30 percent of the family's income, after the income is adjusted for the number of dependents and such items as high medical costs. The Payment Standard can be adjusted by the PHA twice in five years, but cannot exceed the FMR. The voucher amount is thus a fixed value for the family. Because the voucher amount is independent of actual rents in a particular location, it is simpler to administer than Section 8, with its complex FMR standard and annual rent adjustments for the landlords. Because the voucher calculations are only a fraction of the family's income and the fixed local Payment Standard, it is easier for families to move, not just within the city of their PHA's jurisdiction—or even within a single metropolitan area—but anywhere in the U.S. where jobs, educational opportunities, or family or community ties beckon. Project-based programs, such as public housing, do not allow this mobility nor does the Section 8 program.

Closing The Affordability Gap

The major reason for homelessness is the inability to pay for housing; the primary solution to the problem would be to make it affordable. Housing assistance, covering the difference between what families can afford after meeting other basic needs and the cost of renting a suitable unit in the area where they live, should be an entitlement for all who need it.

Homeless households would be enabled to make use of the housing resources in their communities—housing now often underutilized or abandoned because those who need it cannot afford it—if they were given the capacity to pay the initial rent deposit, continuing housing assistance through a rent certificate or voucher, and assistance in the search for housing.

Cushing N. Dolbeare, *Christianity and Crisis*, April 18, 1988.

While a few PHAs have established some Section 8 arrangements to allow limited mobility in a few metropolitan areas, the arrangements involve very complicated contracting, and current law allows HUD only to encourage, not require, PHAs to use certificates in this way. A PHA participating in the voucher program, on the other hand, is required to accept any voucher holder who wishes to move into the PHA's jurisdiction. Currently, however, the overwhelming majority of PHAs do not yet participate in the voucher program; nonparticipating PHAs cannot be required to accept vouchers.

Since the eligible family pays every dollar of the rent above the value of the voucher, the program encourages tenants to bargain with their prospective landlords. This gives the poor family consumer power and thus creates a true housing market. Under Section 8, by contrast, tenants do not care what the rent is, because it is the federal government who pays any rental costs exceeding 30 percent of family income. While the voucher also is designed to enable the family to pay no more than 30 percent of its income for housing in most areas, the family can pay more if it desires. The family also can accept cheaper but sound housing and keep the difference. This too encourages the family to seek out and bargain for the best housing buy at the lowest price. Preliminary figures from the current voucher demonstration indicate that a significant percentage of families—as high as 40 percent—may be able to take advantage of this opportunity to shop around and pay less than 30 percent of their income.

Cutting Housing Costs

Vouchers are also an effective way to reduce the cost of housing to the poor. Private sector costs for building and maintaining housing units are as much as 40 percent lower than public sector costs, because of bureaucratic red tape costs associated with federal programs as well as cost increases rising from Davis-Bacon wage rates and other construction regulations.

Vouchers are the fastest way to house poor families, since vouchers avoid the three to five year lead time required to plan and build new units. And except for New York City and a few other locales, which suffer from rental housing shortages because the supply is artificially constricted by rent and development controls, the private market across the U.S. has created vast supplies of inexpensive, standard quality housing. Indeed, the national vacancy level exceeds 6 percent. Thus there is a plentiful supply of housing to be rented with vouchers.

Criticisms of Vouchers

Most of the criticism of housing vouchers comes from PHAs and so-called tenants' advocates. PHAs resist vouchers because they thereby lose control of housing units; tenants' advocates tend to trust direct government construction programs rather than market situations. What critics of vouchers really seem to be after is a resumption of housing construction programs—despite the huge cost, the delays of such programs, and the fact that building new units could serve only one-third as many families as would be served by vouchers. . . . Congress in 1986 despaired of new construction and diverted funds for new public housing units into modernization of existing public housing units, which are deteriorating and dropping out of the available stock faster than they can be replaced. Such pressure for new construction will continue each year until vouchers are established as a full program and have had a chance to work in harmony with the private market.

The argument against the voucher program [is that] the private market will not provide adequate housing supplies. This is belied by the actual market surpluses of housing. Another argument is that there is a portion of the market that cannot be served by the private market. Here critics point to families with vouchers who are unable or unwilling to locate acceptable units to rent, but such failures to find housing are usually related to renters' intense desire to remain in their current apartments or neighborhoods.

Cheaper and Faster

Vouchers can assist a low-income family for less than half the cost of constructing a new low-income housing unit under other federal housing programs. This means that more than twice as many low-income families can be helped with the same federal outlays spent on new housing. Vouchers also provide immediate assistance to low-income families; by contrast, funding, planning, and construction of new units requires three to five years.

Peter J. Ferrara, The Heritage Foundation *Backgrounder*, September 23, 1988.

Admittedly, minority families and those with many children have experienced greater difficulty in finding new units. But this does not mean that an inherent flaw exists in the voucher program, since exactly these families also are very difficult to serve adequately in other housing programs. Project-based housing programs, for instance, have been plagued with segregation, vandalism, and violence against minority families. All that is needed is an adjustment in the voucher subsidy to account for special needs. In fact, HUD is attempting to compensate for those difficulties by providing increased subsidies for larger families so they can afford larger apartments. HUD is now also paying PHAs a bonus to provide extra help to hard-to-house families.

Improved Mobility

Some PHAs and tenant advocates argue that a voucher system with no limits on mobility will mean that some PHAs will lose vouchers as families leave the jurisdiction, leaving fewer vouchers in these jurisdictions for other families' housing. Given the nature of the congressional system, where representatives are judged by their ability to secure federal largess for their districts, this is a powerful political argument, even though from a national standpoint the housing needs of the total population of poor families are being addressed by vouchers. Simply put, it is impossible to provide mobility without some PHAs losing control over the lives of some resident poor families. But experience indicates that few voucher holders are likely to leave a jurisdiction in any one year.

In response to congressional pressure, HUD has allowed PHAs to limit to 15 percent of their allotment the number of vouchers that can be used by families to move to another jurisdiction. PHAs have been lobbying to reduce the percentage even further. But this would undermine the benefits of improved mobility associated with vouchers. Thus HUD should strenuously oppose any decrease in this percentage when it develops final regulations for a comprehensive program. . . .

An Historic Change

The Administration must establish vouchers as the centerpiece of the nation's low-income housing policy. By giving poor families the right to choose where they live and the incentive to bargain for top value for their rent dollar, vouchers would introduce market pressures, and better rental housing at lower cost to the taxpayer would follow. The improved flexibility and mobility associated with vouchers would help poor families to pursue optimum employment and education opportunities.

A full voucher program would be an historic change in America's low-income housing policy. It would mean a shift from a policy of subsidizing expensive construction to one of helping families to become powerful consumers in the existing and adequate rental market. That change of direction is long overdue.

Distinguishing Between Fact and Opinion

This activity is designed to help develop the basic critical thinking skill of distinguishing between fact and opinion. Consider the following statement as an example: "In 1972, Congress launched the Experimental Housing Allowance Program." This statement is a historical fact that is undeniably true. But consider another statement about the same government program: "The 1972 Experimental Housing Allowance Program was a dismal failure at reducing homelessness." This statement is an opinion with which many people who may favor the program would disagree.

When investigating controversial issues it is important that one be able to distinguish between statements of fact and statements of opinion. It is also important to recognize that not all statements of fact are true. They may appear to be true, but some are based on inaccurate or false information. For this activity, however, we are concerned with understanding the difference between those statements which appear to be factual and those which appear to be based primarily on opinion.

Most of the following statements are taken from the viewpoints in this chapter. Consider each statement carefully. *Mark O for any statement you believe is an opinion or interpretation of facts. Mark F for any statement you believe is a fact.*

If you are doing this activity as a member of a class or group, compare your answers with those of other class or group members. Be able to defend your answers. You may discover that others will come to different conclusions than you. Listening to the reasons others present for their answers may give you valuable insights in distinguishing between fact and opinion.

$$O = opinion$$
$$F = fact$$

205

1. Over 200 communities, including nearly all the major cities on the East and West Coasts, block rent increases.

2. The homelessness of the 1980s seems both qualitatively and quantitatively different from that of earlier times.

3. Today, among the most urgent tasks are to defend rent control and to promote the construction of affordable housing for poor and working-class families.

4. The National Coalition for the Homeless estimates the homeless population at between two and three million.

5. The problem is not too few houses—rather, it is too much government.

6. Between 1970 and 1983, median rents tripled.

7. Only 6 percent of qualifying low- and moderate-income people receive any form of governmental housing assistance.

8. As our nation moves into the next decade, the housing crisis will only worsen.

9. A comprehensive national housing policy along the lines pioneered by Sweden is needed to combat the housing crisis in America.

10. National housing policy in the 1980s was more apt to produce homelessness than homeownership.

11. Ten percent of all the nation's renters whose incomes are less than 50 percent of their area's median live in public housing.

12. The cost of public sector-financed housing typically is 40 percent higher than private costs.

13. The use of housing vouchers is the only current housing strategy that can give poor families the flexibility to pursue jobs.

14. The Section 8 program provides certificates to renters that allow the landlord to obtain a subsidy for housing the certificate holder.

15. Thousands of low-income New York City residents are homeless.

16. Reserving public housing for homeless families will create a demand for homelessness.

Periodical Bibliography

The following articles have been selected to supplement the diverse views presented in this chapter.

Richard P. Appelbaum "The Affordability Gap," *Society*, May/June 1989.

William L. Baer "Haunted Housing," *Reason*, August/September 1989.

Howard Banks "The Low-Income Housing Bind," *Forbes*, August 8, 1988.

Crocker Coulson "The $37,000 Slum," *The New Republic*, January 19, 1987.

Peter Dreier "Communities, Not Carpetbaggers," *The Nation*, August 21-28, 1989.

Judith Ramsey Ehrlich "Homelessness: The Policy Failure Haunting America," *Business Week*, April 25, 1988.

William Greider "America's Desperate Housing Crisis," *Rolling Stone*, December 1, 1988.

Brad Kessler "Down and Out in Suburbia," *The Nation*, September 25, 1989.

Carolyn Lochhead "Door Opening to Dignity," *Insight*, May 16, 1988.

Susan T. Mandel "The Problem at HUD," *National Review*, August 4, 1989.

The New Republic "Abolish HUD," August 21, 1989.

Louis S. Richman "Housing Policy Needs a Rehab," *Fortune*, March 27, 1989.

Mel Settle "Must We Tear Them Down?" *The Humanist*, May/June 1989.

Todd Swanstrom "Homeless: A Product of Policy," *The New York Times*, March 23, 1989.

Ernest van den Haag "Thoughts on Homelessness Today," *The American Spectator*, April 1989.

Camilo José Vergara "Hell in a Very Tall Place," *The Atlantic Monthly*, September 1989.

David Whitman "Down and Out in the 'Path Hotel,'" *U.S. News & World Report*, March 23, 1987.

Organizations to Contact

The editors have compiled the following list of organizations which are concerned with the issues debated in this book. All of them have publications or information available for interested readers. The descriptions are derived from materials provided by the organizations. This list was compiled upon the date of publication. Names and phone numbers of organizations are subject to change.

Catholic Charities USA
1319 F St. NW
Washington, DC 20004
(202) 639-8400

Catholic Charities is a federation of organizations and individuals who carry out the Church's social mission. It provides services such as counseling for the homeless and runs several shelters. Its Commission on Housing publishes periodic updates on housing issues. It also publishes the monthly *Catholic Charities USA*.

Cato Institute
224 Second St. SE
Washington, DC 20003
(202) 546-0200

The Institute sponsors programs designed to assist scholars and laypersons in analyzing public policy questions. It opposes rent control, restrictive zoning laws, and other controls on the housing market. It advocates vouchers to solve the problem of homelessness. Its publications include the book *Rent Control: The Perennial Folly* and the monthlies *Policy Report* and *Cato Journal*.

Center for Community Change Through Housing and Support
University of Vermont
Psychology Department
John Dewey Hall
Burlington, VT 05405-0134
(802) 656-0000

The Center researches the housing and community support needs of people with psychiatric disabilities. It provides technical assistance to state and local agencies and to advocates on developing housing and services to support the mentally ill. Its publications include *Normal Housing with Specialized Supports: A Psychiatric Rehabilitation Approach to Living in the Community*.

Children's Defense Fund (CDF)
122 C St. NW
Washington, DC 20001
(202) 628-8787

CDF advocates programs to prevent teenage pregnancy, family breakdown, family homelessness, and other occurrences which adversely affect children. Their Child Welfare and Mental Health Division has prepared the report *Beyond the Numbers: Homeless Families with Children*. CDF also publishes the monthly newsletter *CDF Reports* and *A Vision for America's Future: An Agenda for the 1990s* which includes a section on homelessness.

Department of Housing and Urban Development (HUD)
451 7th St. SW
Washington, DC 20410
(202) 655-4000

HUD is the federal agency responsible for housing programs and the development and preservation of neighborhoods. For the past several years, it has worked to encourage the private housing market to provide affordable housing for all. It conducts studies on homelessness and related issues, including *The 1988 National Survey of Shelters for the Homeless*.

The Enterprise Foundation
505 American City Building
Columbia, MD 21044
(301) 964-1230

The Foundation helps low-income families purchase their own homes. Participants are required to help rehabilitate houses and to take classes on homeownership. The Foundation publishes the monthly *Network News* and *Cost Cuts*, the quarterly *Networker* to help participants find jobs, and the pamphlet *Lessons of Enterprise*.

Foundation for Economic Education (FEE)
30 S. Broadway
Irvington, NY 10533
(914) 591-7230

This libertarian organization focuses its research on free-market theory and advocates an end to government interference. It believes governmental controls of the housing market, such as rent control and restrictive zoning practices are responsible for the homeless problem. FEE's monthly publication, *The Freeman*, has often covered the issue of homelessness.

Habitat for Humanity International
Habitat and Church Streets
Americus, GA 31709-3498
(912) 924-6935

Habitat is a Christian ministry which seeks to provide decent housing for all. It helps families to construct and purchase their own homes. Habitat is developing position papers on homelessness and affordable housing. It distributes the books *No More Shacks!*, *Love in the Mortar*, and *Kingdom Building: Essays from the Grassroots of Habitat*.

The Heritage Foundation
214 Massachusetts Ave. NW
Washington, DC 20002
(202) 546-4400

The Foundation is a conservative think tank which conducts research on public policy. It advocates free enterprise with limited government involvement, and believes the free market can best meet the housing needs of the homeless. In December 1988 it held a conference on homelessness and published the transcripts in *The Heritage Lectures: Rethinking Policy on Homelessness*. Its occasional publications, the *Backgrounder* and the *Issues Bulletin*, have dealt with homelessness and related issues.

The Homelessness Information Exchange
Community Information Exchange
1830 Connecticut Ave. NW, Fourth Floor
Washington, DC 20009
(202) 462-7551

The Exchange collects and disseminates information on programs for the homeless. It distributes bibliographies on topics such as alternative housing options, advocacy groups, and shelters. It publishes a quarterly newsletter, *Homewords*, and many publications, including *Transitional Housing, Family and Child Homelessness*, and *Helping the Homeless in Your Community*.

Massachusetts Committee for Children and Youth (MCCY)
14 Beacon St., Suite 706
Boston, MA 02108
(617) 742-8555

The Committee conducts research and lobbies to help abused, neglected, and emotionally disturbed children, drug-addicted newborns, adolescents contemplating suicide, and runaway and homeless youth. In 1973 MCCY produced the landmark study *Runaways and Street Children in Massachusetts*. Since then, it has published *Housing Boston's Runaway and Homeless Youth* and *No Place Like Home: A Report on the Tragedy of Homeless Children and Their Families in Massachusetts*.

Mental Health Law Project
2021 L St. NW, Suite 800
Washington, DC 20036-4909
(202) 467-5730

The Project was founded in 1972 to curb abuse and neglect in state mental institutions. Since then, the Project has expanded to include advocacy for the homeless mentally ill. The Project files lawsuits and monitors federal agencies to prevent forced institutionalization of the homeless and to ensure that they receive all the benefits to which they are entitled. The Project makes available copies of staff-written articles, such as "Preventive Commitment: Misconceptions and Pitfalls in Creating a Coercive Community," and "Homeless Mentally Ill People: No Longer Out of Sight and Out of Mind."

National Alliance to End Homelessness, Inc.
1518 K St. NW, Suite 206
Washington, DC 20005
(202) 638-1526

The Alliance works to find permanent solutions to the homeless problem by forming councils of experts on the subject. It publishes the monthly *Alliance* newsletter and a report *Housing and Homelessness*.

National Clearinghouse for Alcohol and Drug Information
PO Box 2345
Rockville, MD 20852
(301) 468-2600

The Clearinghouse distributes information on homelessness as it relates to drug abuse and alcoholism. Its publications include *Homelessness, Health and Human Needs*, and *Homelessness: Alcohol and Other Drugs*.

The National Coalition for the Homeless
1439 Rhode Island Ave. NW
Washington, DC 20005
(202) 659-3310

The Coalition is a federation of organizations concerned about homelessness. It lobbies for more government programs to help the homeless, conducts research, and works as a clearinghouse on information about the homeless. It publishes the monthly newsletter *Safety Network* and many pamphlets, including *Over the Edge: Homeless Families and the Welfare System, Student Resource Guide, Precious Resources: Government-Owned Housing and the Needs of the Homeless*, and *Surplus Properties/Unmet Needs*.

National Housing Institute
439 Main St.
Orange, NJ 07050
(201) 678-3110

The Institute provides training for tenant groups and serves as a resource center on issues such as tenant rights. It supports rent control. It is currently conducting a study of homelessness prevention strategies. It publishes the quarterly *Shelterforce*.

National Institute of Mental Health (NIMH)
Office of Programs for the Homeless Mentally Ill
5600 Fishers Lane, Room 7C-06
Rockville, MD 20857
(301) 443-3706

NIMH conducts research, runs demonstration projects, and provides technical assistance to programs designed to help the homeless mentally ill. It provides bibliographies on homelessness on request. It also publishes *A Synthesis of NIMH-Funded Research Concerning Persons Who Are Homeless and Mentally Ill* and *The Homeless Mentally Ill: Reports Available from the National Institute of Mental Health*.

The National Resource Center on Homelessness and Mental Illness
Policy Research Associates, Inc.
262 Delaware Ave.
Delmar, NY 12054
(800) 444-7415

The Center disseminates information on mental health as it relates to homelessness. The Center maintains a database of information on the homeless mentally ill. It will provide free information packets on request. It publishes the quarterly *Access*.

Self-Help Enterprises (SHE)
PO Box 351
220 S. Bridge St.
Visalia, CA 93279
(209) 733-9091

SHE has helped 3,300 low-income families, mostly farmworkers, to build their own homes. SHE publishes the pamphlet *Self-Help Enterprises* and the booklet *Working Together: Twenty Years of Self-Help Enterprises*.

Urban Homesteading Assistance Board
40 Prince St.
New York, NY 10012
(212) 226-4119

The Board consists of low-income neighborhood housing groups and tenant organizations dedicated to developing resident-controlled housing. It helps to develop homesteading projects throughout New York City. It publishes *City Limits— The News Magazine of New York City Housing and Neighborhoods* ten times a year, as well as *Current Programs and Projects*.

Bibliography of Books

Alliance Housing Council — *Housing and Homelessness*. Washington, DC: National Alliance to End Homelessness, 1988.

Charles W. Baird — *Rent Control: The Perennial Folly*. San Francisco: Cato Institute, 1980.

Richard D. Bingham, Roy E. Green, and Sammis B. White, eds. — *The Homeless in Contemporary Society*. Newbury Park, CA: Sage Publications, Inc., 1987.

Rachel Bratt — *Rebuilding a Low-Income Housing Policy*. Philadelphia: Temple University Press, 1989.

Steve Burghardt and Michael Fabricant — *Working Under the Safety Net*. Newbury Park, CA: Sage Publications, Inc., 1987.

Ann Cibulski and Charles Hoch — *Homelessness: An Annotated Bibliography*. Chicago: CPL Bibliographies, 1986.

Department of Housing and Urban Development — *Homelessness in America*. Washington, DC: Department of Housing and Urban Development, 1984.

Department of Housing and Urban Development — *Housing America: Freeing the Spirit of Enterprise*. Washington, DC: Department of Housing and Urban Development, 1987.

Nathan Glazer — *The Limits of Social Policy*. Cambridge, MA: Harvard University Press, 1988.

The Heritage Foundation — *The Heritage Lectures: Rethinking Policy on Homelessness*. Washington, DC: The Heritage Foundation, 1989. Pamphlet available from The Heritage Foundation, 214 Massachusetts Ave. NE, Washington, DC 20002.

Marjorie Hope and James Young — *The Faces of Homelessness*. Lexington, MA: Lexington Books, 1986.

Anna Kosof — *Homeless in America*. New York: Franklin Watts Inc., 1988.

Jonathan Kozol — *Rachel and Her Children*. New York: Crown Publishers, 1988.

H. Richard Lamb, ed. — *The Homeless Mentally Ill: A Task Force Report of the American Psychiatric Association*. Washington, DC: The American Psychiatric Press Inc., 1984.

Richard H. Ropers — *The Invisible Homeless: A New Urban Ecology*. New York: Human Sciences Press, 1988.

Peter Rossi — *Down and Out in America: The Origins of Homelessness*. Chicago: University of Chicago Press, 1989.

E. Fuller Torrey — *Nowhere to Go: The Tragic Odyssey of the Homeless Mentally Ill*. New York: Harper & Row, 1988.

William Tucker — *The Excluded Americans: Homelessness and Housing Policies*. Washington, DC: Regnery Gateway, 1989.

Irving Welfeld — *Where We Live*. New York: Simon & Schuster, 1988.

Index

Aid to Families with Dependent
Children (AFDC), 18, 108, 109
alcoholism, *see* substance abuse
American Civil Liberties Union
(ACLU), 130, 131
American Psychiatric Association, 18, 56
Appelbaum, Paul S., 131, 135
Appelbaum, Richard P., 150, 171,
172, 193
Association of Community
Organizations for Reform Now
(ACORN), 175, 177-179, 181, 182,
188
Atlas, John, 152, 168, 170

Barna, Barbara, 176
Bassuk, Ellen, 35, 73, 139
Beirne, Kenneth J., 100, 102, 104,
197
Brown, Joyce, 130-132, 136
Bush administration, 173
Bykofsky, Stuart D., 40, 45, 48

Chapman, Stephen, 133
Cohen, Carl I., 75
Community Development Block
Grant (CDBG), 103-104
Community for Creative Non-
Violence (CCNV), 22, 23-25
Conway, Edwin M., 117
Crocker, C. Brandon, 112

Dear, Michael J., 137, 139, 143
deinstitutionalization, *see* mental
illness
divorce, *see* family breakdown
Dolbeare, Cushing N., 201
Dreier, Peter, 152, 168, 170
drug abuse, *see* substance abuse

economic factors
and deindustrialization, 84, 85
cause homelessness, 65-70, 81-87,
99, 107, 108
con, 113-114
inflation's role in, 19, 66, 68, 108,
109
Experimental Housing Allowance
Program (EHAP), 199

family breakdown
and substance abuse, 77

causes homelessness, 19, 35-36, 70,
71-74, 114, 128, 136
Ferguson, Sarah, 180
Ferlauto, Richard C., 108, 191
Ferrara, Peter J., 203
Foscarinis, Maria, 25-26, 32, 36-37
Friends Committee on National
Legislation, 85

gentrification, 61, 62, 63, 68-69, 176
Gilderbloom, John I., 150, 171, 172

Heatherly, Charles L., 199
Hirsch, Eric, 174, 178
Hoch, Charles, 123
Hoffman, Daniel N., 108, 191
Hombs, Mary Ellen, 17, 23-24
homeless
as serious problem, 17-20, 33, 76,
84, 94
con, 21-27, 101, 102-103
difficulty in assessing, 113, 118,
139-140, 157
threatens families, 28-33, 76, 94
myth of, 34-38
causes of
alcoholism, 75-80
economic factors, 81-87
family breakdown, 71-74
lack of housing, 65-70
characteristics of, 44
age, 18, 42, 43, 108, 140
crime records, 70, 102, 140
health, 33, 43, 61-62, 80, 140
race, 30, 35, 86, 94, 109
chemical dependency among,
35-36, 42, 44, 70, 76-80
programs for, 120
rate of, 23, 37, 119
deserve sympathy, 39-45
con, 40, 46-49
history of, 82-84, 126
impact of
destabilizes communities, 47-49
psychological reactions to, 20, 43,
62, 97
job training programs for, 96, 122
media coverage of, 22, 66-67, 76,
98, 103, 157
mental illness among, 56-59, 62-63,
94, 114

and institutionalization
  as necessary, 40, 115, 129-136
  con, 56, 137-144
programs for, 18, 56, 57, 59, 120,
  134
protests by, 86-87, 94, 177
teenagers, 42
unemployment among, 23, 44-45,
  94
veterans, 43-44, 94
Horowitz, Carl F., 21
housing
  cooperatives, 152-154
  gentrification's effect on, 61, 62, 63,
    68-69, 176
  homesteading programs, 154-155,
    177-178, 179-182
  low-income, 18, 61, 62, 68-69, 101,
    151
  Section 8 program, 193-194, 195,
    200, 201, 202
  shortage of
    causes homelessness, 18, 61,
      62-63, 65-70, 80, 104, 108
    con, 162, 164-165
    governmental response to
      national program needed, 99,
        150-155
      con, 156-160
    should subsidize construction,
      70, 82, 94, 98-99, 120, 191-196
      con, 152, 155, 198, 202
    reasons for
      inflation, 19, 66, 68, 108
      land prices, 172
      private market's failure, 84-85,
        95, 96, 151-152, 155
        con, 26-27, 194-195, 203
      regulations, 101, 104, 158-160,
        163-167
        con, 151
      rent control, 104, 158, 161-167
        con, 151, 168-173
      tax policies, 151, 152, 172, 173
      zoning laws, 172
  single-room occupancy (SRO)
    destruction of, 18, 63, 68, 101,
      120, 124, 158
    should be replenished, 104-105
  vacancy rates, 60, 104, 157-158,
    175, 176, 184
  vouchers, 105, 197-204

Idelson, Chuck, 172
immigration, illegal, 162
inflation
  and rent control, 166

causes homelessness, 19, 66, 68
effects on welfare benefits, 108,
  109

Kondratas, Anna, 25, 36, 160
Kozol, Jonathan, 28, 35, 36, 43, 60
Krauthammer, Charles, 129

Lam, Julie A., 65
Lamb, H. Richard, 55
Lauriat, Alison S., 73
Leo, John, 46

McKinney Act, 94, 171
McMurry, Dan, 71
Magnet, Myron, 114
Marcuse, Peter, 81, 93
Mehrten, Joseph, 156
mental illness
  causes homelessness, 55-59, 80
  con, 60-64, 74, 162
  in families, 35, 36
mentally ill people
  are mislabeled, 61-64
  community care for, 120, 138, 139,
    140
    is insufficient, 18, 56-57, 58-59,
      61, 101, 134
    objections to, 134, 142-143
  number of homeless, 18, 35, 37-38,
    44, 62-63, 70, 119
  should be institutionalized, 40, 115,
    129-136
    con, 56, 137-144
Mutual Housing Association of New
  York (MHANY), 175, 179-182

National Coalition for the Homeless,
  37-38, 94, 139-140, 169
National Health Care for the
  Homeless Program (HCH), 41-42

Pines, Burton Yale, 199
poverty
  causes homelessness, 61, 78, 80,
    107, 201
  con, 74
  inflation exacerbates, 19, 66, 68
Proch, Kathleen, 121
public housing,
  18, 61, 62, 68-69, 101, 151,
    191-196

Reagan administration
  attitude toward homeless, 96, 102
  budget cuts by, 24, 66, 96
    caused homelessness, 113
    of housing subsidies, 18, 162, 176,
      192

rent control
  causes homelessness, 104, 158,
    161-167
  con, 151, 168-173
Robinson, Elzie, 185, 189-190
Ropers, Richard H., 62
Rossi, Peter, 77, 106
Rubin, Leonore, 73

Schwartz, David C., 108, 191
shelters
  are inadequate, 49, 56, 94-95, 121,
    123-128
  community objections to, 95, 126
  cost of, 49
  for mentally ill people, 18, 56
  government should support,
    117-122
  con, 125-126, 127-128
  increased numbers of, 101, 103,
    124, 125
single-room occupancy (SRO)
  housing
  destruction of, 18, 63, 68, 101, 120,
    124, 158
  families' use of, 125
  should be replenished, 104-105
Slayton, Robert A., 123
Snyder, Mitch, 17, 23-24, 25, 26, 27
social programs
  AFDC, 18, 108, 109
  are insufficient, 18, 43, 96, 106-111
  con, 112-116
  for mentally ill, 120, 138, 139, 140,
    142-144
  are insufficient, 18, 56-57, 58-59,
    61, 101, 134
  inflation's effect on, 108, 109
  job skills training, 96, 122
  old age pensions, 108
  would help the homeless, 18, 96,
    106-111
  con, 112-116
Sokolovsky, Jay, 75
squatting
  should be allowed, 174-182
  con, 183-190
Stark, Louisa, 64
Stefl, Mary E., 19
Stengel, Richard, 141
substance abuse, 35, 36
  among homeless people, 40, 42, 44, 70
  amount of, 23, 37, 38, 119

as cause of, 18, 75-80
  con, 74
among mentally ill, 58
programs for, 120
reasons for, 77, 78-79
Supplemental Security Income (SSI),
  18, 58, 119
Swanstrom, Todd, 69

Taber, Merlin A., 121
Talbott, John A., 55
Torrey, E. Fuller, 57
Tsakopoulos, Angelo, 159-160
Tucker, William, 158, 161, 163, 165,
  170, 172, 185, 189

unemployment
  and substance abuse, 77, 80
  causes homelessness, 18-19, 30,
    31-33, 41, 94, 136
  con, 85, 113, 162, 164-165
  deindustrialization and, 61, 84, 85
United Nations Commission on
  Human Settlements, 157
United States
  Department of Defense, 104
  Department of Housing and Urban
    Development (HUD), 171, 192,
    193
  budget cuts and, 27
  emergency housing programs, 104
  surveys by, 24, 25, 101-102, 103,
    113, 119, 139, 164
  government's response to homeless
    is adequate, 100-105
    con, 19-20, 94-98, 175-176
    is needed, 20, 93-99, 107, 111,
      175
    con, 26-27, 49
  local, 101, 102, 104-105
United States Conference of Mayors,
  23, 37, 76
Urban Institute, 25, 172

Weber, Peter, 183
welfare, see social programs
Whitman, David, 34, 158
Whittemore, Hank, 32
Wolch, Jennifer R., 137, 139, 143
Wood, Peter, 174, 178
Wright, James D., 39, 65

zoning restrictions, 151, 159, 160,
  163, 172

215